## About the Author

Andrew Crofts has been a freelance writer for over 35 years and is one of Britain's most successful ghostwriters. He has written over 30 books and also works as a freelance journalist, business writer, novelist and non-fiction author. He is in demand by famous personalities as well as leading businessmen and his books include several bestsellers.

ANDREW CROFTS

# THE FREELANCE WRITER'S HANDBOOK

## How to make money and enjoy your life

PIATKUS

# 🎗 Visit the Piatkus website!

Piatkus publishes a wide range of bestselling fiction and non-fiction, including books on health, mind, body & spirit, sex, self-help, cookery, biography and the paranormal.

If you want to:
- read descriptions of our popular titles
- buy our books over the internet
- take advantage of our special offers
- enter our monthly competition
- learn more about your favourite Piatkus authors

VISIT OUR WEBSITE AT: **www.piatkus.co.uk**

Copyright © 2002 by Andrew Crofts

First published in Great Britain in 2002 by
Judy Piatkus (Publishers) Ltd
5 Windmill Street
London W1T 2JA
email: info@piatkus.co.uk

Reprinted 2003

**The moral right of the author has been asserted**

*A catalogue record for this book is*
*available from the British Library*

ISBN 0 7499 2309 1

This book has been printed on paper manufactured
with respect for the environment using wood from
managed sustainable resources

Typeset by Action Publishing Technology, Gloucester
Printed and bound in Great Britain by
Biddles Ltd, *www.biddles.co.uk*

To my wife, Susan, with much love and many thanks for putting up the vicissitudes of a freelance life.

# Contents

# Introduction

Freelance writing is the most wonderful way of earning a living. Nothing, except perhaps inherited wealth, provides greater personal freedom.

You can follow your interests and develop yourself in any direction you choose, free to live where and how you want, and to travel wherever and whenever the urge takes you. As a freelancer you never know when Lady Luck is going to drop some fabulous opportunity into your lap.

My aim is to inspire you with the necessary hope, ambition and nerve to give it a go, and to lead you through the various preparation stages so that you have a sensible, realistic plan and an understanding of the marketplace you're about to enter.

I will then show you how to turn your writing skills into a business that will support you in whatever lifestyle you've set your heart on.

There are many ways to make a decent and pleasant living from writing, but it's all too easy to be carried away by unrealistic dreams. We all need dreams to get us out of bed in the mornings, but to make them come true we must have the basic tools of our profession. Becoming a successful freelance writer is difficult, but it's perfectly doable if you go about it the right way. I'll show you how to put yourself in a position to be offered the lucky breaks, then all you'll need do to succeed is produce the best work you're capable of.

Much of it is about marketing. Selling writing skills is not a lot different to selling airline seats, vodka or cigarettes.

Approach your career as you might approach the launch of a new shop or a new pop singer. I'm going to show you how to find customers, persuade them to buy from you for the first time and how to keep them coming back for more.

Every morning you wake up as a freelance you know something exciting might happen today. A publisher may ring with a big commission, your novel might be accepted, a huge star might agree to an interview, a magazine might buy an article or send you to Tahiti with all expenses paid, the film rights to a book could sell for thousands or a chat show host will want to interview you. Most days none of these things will happen, but some days they will.

My book *How to Make Money from Freelance Writing* came out at the beginning of the nineties. Five years later it was updated to include developments such as word processors and fax machines. But the past five years have brought changes so dramatic in the world of freelance writing that only a science-fiction author could have predicted them.

Not only have we seen the arrival of stars like John Grisham and J.K. Rowling, but there has also been the spread of the Internet, the growing use of e-mail and mobile phones, the introduction of 'print on demand', online publishing, e-zines, laptops and the rest. I've also been in the business ten years longer and have learnt a great deal more. So I decided to rewrite the book from start to finish.

In the past thirty years, ever since I left school, I've tried to sell work in virtually every area of the writing market. Some attempts were more successful than others. I've collected as many rejections and disappointments as anyone. But I've still managed to stay in business and I still wouldn't trade writing for any other profession. I hope this book will lead you to not only making a good living, but to having a great deal of fun doing so. If you persevere you can achieve whatever you want.

# CHAPTER ONE

# Why Do It?

*'Almost anyone can be an author; the business is to collect money and fame from this state of being.'*
A.A. Milne

Being a writer means you can dip into interesting and exciting lives and situations, find out whatever you want, and then return to the peace and security of your own garret to write the resulting story, whether it be a book, a film script or an article for the local newspaper.

You can live as many different lives as you want, while always maintaining an escape route. You can follow any path your curiosity takes you down, and go to places you'd never otherwise see; one day rubbing shoulders with princes at polo matches, the next unearthing a prostitution racket in a Third World shanty town or taking tea with your local vicar.

Since stories that sell have to be interesting, we who create them need only go out into the world when there's something interesting to see, do or learn. The rest of the time we can relax in the comfort of our own home, tapping away on the keyboard, or putting our feet up with a newspaper.

Provided we create, in a professional manner, a product that editors, publishers, producers and readers want to buy, we're free of all other obligations; and greater freedom, I believe, is pretty much the goal for all of us.

## Getting a Private Life

How often have you heard someone regretting that they don't spend more time with their family and friends? That they're always too busy to watch their children's football or netball matches or school plays. Then there are the home deliveries that require a day off work, along with the anniversaries, birthdays and other family occasions that cause endless ill feeling when they're missed because of pressure of work.

Freelance writers can spend as much time as we like with our loved ones because our working schedules can nearly always be fitted around other arrangements. If your day is full of school runs or the preparation of meals there's always the early morning or the evening to do the work. If you like to lie in in the morning, then you can work in the evening. If you're an early riser you can have your whole working day over and done with by the time late risers are finishing their breakfast. We have more control over our private lives than almost any other kind of worker.

## Live and Work Wherever You Choose

Since you'll be working at home for at least fifty per cent of the time, it doesn't matter where you live. You can secrete yourself in a converted lighthouse in Cornwall, a loft in London's Docklands or a beach house in Bali as long as you have access to a computer and a telephone. Of course, it'll depend a little on where you have to get to for your research, but I'll cover that in more detail later. There are stories to be had in every possible location; but, when the world is your oyster, the biggest difficulty may just be choosing.

## Exploiting the Golden Age of the Writer

Some believe we're entering the age of the philistine; that all the great writing is in the past. I believe the opposite.

We're now entering the age of the 'information provider', which is basically the techie's term for writer. Imagine what a time Charles Dickens would be having if he were alive now and writing for *EastEnders*. Imagine the enormous 'new age' and self-help publishing markets that would be available to the Ancient Greek philosophers if they were propounding their theories today.

The opportunities for writers on the Internet are only just emerging. It is the biggest and fastest-growing marketplace ever. With the arrival of the information age, the production of words has become faster and consequently more plentiful. So we see a great deal of mediocre material, which disguises the fact that people are still producing great writing; it's just harder to spot it among everything else.

For professional writers the quantity of work available is almost as important as the quality. We all struggle to write as well as we can, but to support ourselves we need a regular supply of outlets. It would be nice to spend years perfecting literary masterpieces before presenting them to the marketplace. The reality is we do the best we can and now and then a masterpiece pops out.

To earn a living you must have a craft you can peddle. The people most in demand are those who can create something everyone else needs. Before the internal combustion engine the blacksmith was in that enviable position. Freelance plumbers and electricians can always find work if they go about looking for it in the right way, just like self-employed lawyers and accountants.

We're currently entering a golden period for the skilled purveyors of information – writers – and anyone who has developed the craft to a professional standard will have a skill they can continue developing and selling all their life.

## Ride That Learning Curve

One of the great joys in life is learning new things. It's why writers are in business; because we teach people things they want to learn. The learning curve for the writer is steeper and longer than anyone else's because we're constantly moving on to new material and having to master it to a high enough standard to pass it on. Unless you're going to write about one subject only, which is a perfectly valid thing to do if you can earn enough money from it, you will constantly be increasing your knowledge of the world around you. Even if you do specialise in one subject, writing about it will not only allow you to deepen that specialist knowledge, but also to hone your ability to communicate.

Since staleness and boredom are two of the greatest obstacles to job satisfaction, the life-long learning curve is another powerful perk for professional writers.

## Satisfying Your Ego

There is a buzz to be had from seeing your name in print – particularly at the beginning of your career. We all benefit from the odd ego boost. There is still a certain kudos to being a writer, a hangover perhaps from the days when only a small percentage of the population was able to read and write. We all benefit from the reflected prestige of Booker Prize novels and Pulitzer Prize-winning journalism.

# CHAPTER TWO

# Do You Have What it Takes?

*'Be a scribe! Your body will be sleek, your hand will be soft ... You are one who sits grandly in your house; your servants answer speedily; beer is poured copiously; all who see you rejoice in good cheer. Happy is the heart of him who writes; he is young each day.'*

Ptahotep, 4500 BC

Writing is a hard profession, but the rewards are more than worth the struggle. What prize was ever worth having without a fight?

Freelance writing is one of the most competitive marketplaces ever devised; almost up there with wanting to join the SAS or a million-selling pop band. Before you put your fingers up to your boss or circulate indecent pictures of him through the company e-mail, let's just check that you understand what you're letting yourself in for.

## Surviving Early Starvation

Although I'll be suggesting ways of structuring the early stages of your career, there will be lean years at the beginning as you establish a reputation and create a body of work to sell. There may be times when no money comes in for several months. Can you live with that sort of uncertainty?

If you're currently on a fat salary, with a fat mortgage and dependent family, you need to think carefully about how you're going to make the transition. If, however, you're young, have no dependants, or are reasonably financially secure, then you've passed the first obstacle.

## Are You Really Nosy and Hopeless at Keeping Secrets?

Do you want to know how the world works and why? Do you always want to ask impertinent questions the moment you meet people? Are you desperate to know how situations came about and where they might be leading to? Are you an avid gossip? Do you love to tell stories and amaze people with facts you've discovered?

To make it as a writer you must be all these things and more.

Nothing whets my appetite more than a foreign accent on the phone, offering to let me into the secrets from some world I've never visited before, revealing scandals in high places or adventures in low ones, inspirational emotional journeys or mighty physical feats. I want to know what it feels like to be an enforced child bride, a great courtesan, a spy or a murderer, or to have been present at some great moment in history. I want to find out every detail and then tell as many people as I can persuade to listen.

If you're secretive by nature you'll never make a writer. (There are exceptions, like J.D. Salinger, but you'd have to strike it very lucky to have a career break like *Catcher in the Rye*.) You must be desperate to enlighten and amaze your readers.

## Learning to Bear Rejection

We all get rejected at some stage, whether it's by someone we try to chat up or a boss we want to impress, but few have to face rejection on such a regular basis as a writer.

It always stings to have your efforts rebuffed, insulted or ignored. Later in the book I'll describe ways to soften the blows, but they will come. Most of us have heard the stories of the famous best-seller being rejected (there are publishers who turned down *Harry Potter*, just as there are record companies that turned down the Beatles) and most of the things you'll write will be rejected by at least ten people before one buys them.

Will you be able to handle that?

## Do You Have a Will of Iron?

All freelancers need self-discipline. Will you be able to make yourself go out after stories and then sit down at the computer for eight hours a day, or whatever it takes to get the work out on time?

If you're working at home you'll have to be able to ignore the domestic distractions. Can you resist the dog's requests to be walked? The children's requests to be taken out or your partner's suggestion to go upstairs for an 'afternoon kip'? Many of these things will be part of your new lifestyle choices, but can you stop yourself from filling the entire day with distractions, leaving no time for the actual work needed to pay for them?

Fear of hunger will, of course, help to motivate you, as will fear of missed deadlines or fear of failure. Only you know if they will be enough to make you competitive.

## Do You Enjoy Your Own Company?

Writers need to be comfortable with their own company much of the time. If you live in a family home the solitude will be lessened by the sounds of family life going on outside the office door, but you'll still be spending most of the time living inside your head, with nothing but a screen for company. There'll be the forays into the outside world to gather material, of course, but you'll be operating as a lone hunter most of the time.

For most writers, I suspect, the solitude is one of the reasons they choose the job in the first place.

## Can You See Sense in the Chaos?

Can you structure stories from material that others see as unrelated and random? Can you piece together ideas and evidence, quotes, facts and opinions and make some sense of them, forging connections and drawing parallels so that your readers finish up seeing things differently, learning something new, understanding things that previously baffled them?

To be a writer you need to be able to see the wood for the trees.

## Are You Good at Persevering?

The most successful writers are often those left in the race when everyone else has given up. If there were one golden rule for success it would be: *'Never, never, never give up.'*

## Could You Sell Ice to Eskimos?

Assuming you can write well, the question is, can you sell what you've written?

Can you package an idea in a few words and convince a busy editor, publisher or film producer that they want to know more? Can you make them willing to part with their money just to find out more about what you have to say?

Hollywood producers are reputed to ask writers to 'give me the story in twenty-five words'. Any project, whether it's fact or fiction, should be capable of being distilled down to one or two sentences. You're going to be selling your material to people who have a million things they'd rather be doing than reading what you've written or listening to what you have to say.

For book and film writers there are agents who'll do some of the selling for you (see Chapter Nineteen), and many writers would no more make a selling call than give away their children, but a knowledge of marketing will always help.

## Are You a Good Listener?

A few writers are able to use their egos as their material. Columnists in newspapers, for instance, and critics and experts in specialised fields. To move into areas outside your own opinions and experience, however, it's useful to be able to suppress your own ego and let the subject do the talking.

If you're writing about a gangster it's pointless telling him he should be ashamed of himself. Do that and he'll clam up and tell you nothing (if he doesn't hit you). If you want your subjects to shine, expand and possibly even give themselves away, you must be willing to put your questions, sit back and listen.

Being a good listener is one of the most useful attributes a writer can have. If you always need to be the centre of attention you may be able to make a living from your words, but you'll always be limited in what you can write about.

Subjects of interviews are often shocked to find that a journalist who seemed so nice during the interview went away and wrote something cruel. The subject probably liked the writer because they didn't say much, just allowed them to ramble on. The subject was lulled into a sense of security and probably gave away more than they meant to. The writer had succeeded in the first part of their job. They then did the other part, passing that material on to the reader. If they'd told the subject they didn't like them or disagreed with them, then the subject would have changed tack, put on an act, covered up the truth, and the journalist would have been less successful.

I'll be looking at interview skills in more detail later (see Chapter Seven).

## What Are the Entry Requirements?

You don't need qualifications to get into this marketplace. Many freelance writers start out as employees of newspapers or broadcasting organisations, gaining the work experience they need to launch themselves. To get those jobs you need to compete at the interview stage, so it probably helps to have some sort of higher education in English, or perhaps a degree in media studies or journalism. But even then practical work will count for more. Someone who's been out into the world, written stories and had them published will always be miles ahead of someone who only has academic qualifications.

If you tell people you're a freelance writer, that's what you are. Then all you have to do to prove it is show them something you've written and sold.

The writing correspondence courses advertised in the press will point you in the right direction creatively, and will give you some tips on how to sell your work. More importantly, they may give you the self-confidence you need to take the first step into the profession.

The fact that you've done one of these courses, however, will not impress anyone in the profession. In fact, it may mark you out as an amateur and count against you. By all means take one if you feel it will help, but keep quiet about it. Only you know if you feel ready to be a professional and start submitting work. If you believe you still need a little help then any course or self-help book may be able to give you the boost you need. Try as many of them as you can afford.

But since the only entry requirement for the marketplace is to have sold something, let's work out how you're going to do that.

# CHAPTER THREE

# Getting Started

*'Write without pay until somebody offers pay.'*　　　Mark Twain

Seeing where to start is the hardest thing to do. In this chapter I want to help you decide where it is you want to get to in your professional life, and then show you how you can make a start today, using what you already know.

Starting as a writer is a Catch-22 situation. You need experience to convince people you can write, but you need to have been published to convince people to give you that experience. That means you're going to have to do a lot of work on spec, and you're going to have to accept that much of it will never be published. Look upon it as serving an apprenticeship.

Make two lists. First, subjects you know something about. Then, media that might be interested in buying articles on these subjects. Don't throw your hands up in modest horror and say you know nothing and have done nothing that could be of interest to anyone. Everyone has some sort of knowledge or experience that, with a little honing, can be packaged and sold.

Let's invent a few would-be writers and see what they could be doing to get started.

### Humphrey

Because he couldn't think what else to do, Humphrey is reading business studies at university.

Humphrey could write about:

- Choosing a degree subject.

- The pressures of school examinations on young people.

- How to choose a university.

- What to do if you get turned down.

- The pros and cons of university education.

- The differences between school life and university life.

- A practical guide to surviving on a budget and where to get your washing done.

- How to find accommodation in a city miles from home.

- A student's-eye view of sex, drugs and rock 'n' roll.

- Holiday jobs and what they pay.

- Student travel and how to organise it.

- Does a business studies course prepare you for the real world of business?

Some of these topics he might be able to write about off the top of his head; others might require him to ask a few of his colleagues for quotes, opinions and experiences.

Where might Humphrey sell his work?

He could start with his university's magazines, of which there are bound to be several. If he's very entrepreneurial he could even start his own, using college equipment. He could also go to the local papers in both his university town and his home town.

Next he could approach the education supplements of all the national papers and magazines. He could search for e-zines on the Web, especially those dedicated to student life. He could approach local radio stations with suggestions for talks or monologues on his list of subjects. He could start thinking about a book entitled *A Guide to Being a Student* which could be marketed to those in their final year of school.

## Jackie

Soon after leaving school, Jackie married and started a family and has spent virtually every waking moment since then tending to housework or small children. She thinks she has no experience and nothing to say that would interest anyone. She's entirely wrong. Parenthood is a state that will attack most people at some stage and anyone who can report from the front line has valuable information.

What could Jackie write about?

- What it feels like to be a young mum stuck at home when your peer group are out clubbing and getting their careers launched.

- Ten top tips for having a baby and retaining your sanity.

- A survey of local pubs and restaurants and how child-friendly they are.

- How to persuade a working partner they have to pull their weight when they get home after a 'hard day at the office'.

- How to choose good babysitters, childminders or playgroups.

- Preparing yourself to do things other than raise children.

- How to cook for a young family without using fish fingers.

- How to throw children's parties without wrecking your house.

- Twenty things to do with small children on a wet winter's afternoon.

Like Humphrey, Jackie could probably write some of these pieces off the top of her head, but she'll also have access to any number of other new mothers through the local baby-network, all of whom will be brimming with opinions and anecdotes about their experiences.

Where could Jackie sell her work?

There are plenty of magazines aimed directly at parents of young children, newly-weds and women in general. The subjects that Jackie has experience in are of interest to all of them. She could also write about designing and furnishing a nursery for a homes magazine or making children's birthday cakes for a cookery magazine. She could put together a book of the hundred biggest mistakes people make when they have their first baby.

## John

After going into the profession straight from school, John has been an accountant for twenty years. Everyone he knows makes jokes about how boring his job is and he has started to believe them. How could be possibly have anything to write about?

What could John write about? Like parenting, managing money is a subject few of us can avoid. John could offer advice on virtually every aspect of personal finance. He has his own and colleagues' experience to draw on, and he probably has a pile of reference books at the office which answer all the questions commonly asked of accountants:

- How much should I be saving in a pension to give me a secure old age?

- How much does it cost to privately educate my children and how can I raise the money?

- What are the ten most important facts to remember if I'm starting a business of my own?

- Is it more tax-efficient for a working couple to get married or stay single?

- What are the five best things you can do with a £1000 windfall?

- How everyone can cut their overheads by twenty-five per cent.

- How to give money to your grandchildren tax-efficiently.

Who could John sell his ideas to?

The list of potential subjects is endless and so is the list of people who will buy them. He could have a regular column in a local paper giving financial advice. He could provide pension and budgeting advice in a retirement magazine. He could write about mortgages in a homes magazine or student finance in a university publication or handling charitable funds in a parish magazine. He could write a book on how to manage your finances successfully.

## Caroline

After working for thirty years as a human resources director in a large company, Caroline has retired at fifty. She's married but doesn't have children, so she's free to please herself as to how she spends the second half of her career.

What could Caroline write about? To begin with she could draw on her years in HR. She's spent thirty years studying companies and people, both of which are subjects of endless fascination.

She could write:

- Articles for young people on how to impress potential employers at interviews.

- Articles for older people on how to prepare themselves for retirement so they get the best deal possible.

- Articles for senior management on how to recruit the best staff and keep them motivated.

- Articles about women going back to work after maternity breaks, or for people thinking about making mid-career changes.

She could also write about her own experience (and that of others she knows) of taking early retirement. Is it a wise move or a potential route to an early grave? Should you consider moving to a sunnier (or cheaper) country?

Who could Caroline sell her work to?

The subjects that she has experience of can be adapted to fit almost anyone. She could write a careers advice column in a local paper or young people's magazine. She could write for retirement magazines or company in-house publications. She could prepare a book on early retirement and how to get the most from it.

## What Do You Want from Life as a Writer?

Before you can reach your goal you have to decide what it is.

Do you want to be a great literary novelist?

Do you want to travel the world and be paid for it?

Do you want to stay at home and write about gardening or bee-keeping?

Do you want to become known as an expert on one particular subject, or do you just want to follow your own interests wherever they might lead you?

Do you want to have a regular column in a newspaper or do you want to be a writer on a soap opera?

Do you want to live a hermit-like existence on a small Scottish island or be part of the international jet set, partying with Formula One racing drivers and supermodels?

You might be happy with any of these options, and there's no reason why you can't pursue all of them if you have sufficient time and energy, but it would probably be wise to have a priority list. There's no reason why you shouldn't change and adapt this list as you learn of new options and possibilities, but it always helps to have at least some sort of map for the future. Even if you're not yet quite sure how you're going to get there.

If you're going to be a writer you'll have to have something to write about. So how do you want to spend your time when you're not writing? If you enjoy doing up houses, then do that and pass your skills on to readers. Gardening? The same applies. In fact, there's probably no subject on earth that can't be written about by someone who knows what they're talking about. That doesn't mean you have to be an expert. You might just want to go skiing once and write a piece about being a novice on the slopes, or you might want to build a pond in your garden and recoup some of the costs by writing about the experience. The chances that you will have anything interesting to say to anyone will decrease dramatically with every hour you sit in your office staring out of the window, or on the sofa staring at the television.

## What Do You Know Already?

When you tell people what you do for a living, what questions do they ask?

If you're a doctor they may ask you about pain in their back – so write about it. For a solicitor it might be advice on their house purchase or their divorce. If you're a dustman they might ask about the weirdest things you've found in a bin. A chambermaid could write about things that people do to hotel rooms and a nurse could write about the ten corniest chat-up lines that patients come out with.

A gardener will be asked what plants do well in what conditions and how to keep them healthy. How to achieve dramatic effects in small gardens, or how to design large gardens to be low maintenance. They'll be asked for tips about buying lawn mowers and pruning trees, laying terraces and building ponds, growing flowers for the house and building climbing frames.

If you're a hairdresser people will want to know how to keep their hair healthy, how to choose a style to suit their faces or how to choose a hairdresser. If you're a beautician they'll ask how to stop biting their nails, what colours they should paint them to suit their clothes, how to improve their complexions, how to cover up spots.

These, and many more professions, can all provide subjects for articles, and this material could be built up for books or radio or television shows. The fact that they've been done before doesn't matter – people will always keep asking the same questions and a subject will be constantly developing.

## How Can You Build on It?

Much of this you'll hold in your head or be able to look up in reference books. You can also research it easily by talking to colleagues. Become as expert in your field as you can. Jackie, for instance, should read as many mother and baby books and magazines as possible to get a rounded picture of the market and the style people write in, increasing her knowledge and coming up with ideas. John, the accountant, should read all the 'Your Money' sections of the papers, particularly the letters columns, to understand the sorts of problems that people have and the information they're looking for.

## Look for Topical Angles

It will always help if you ally your personal expertise to something in the news. If there's a lot of talk about an economic slowdown in the papers, then John could offer pieces on 'How to Survive a Recession'. If there's been controversy about single mothers and how hard it is for them to cope, Jackie could write an article on the difficulties of dealing with a child who doesn't sleep, angling specifically to one-parent families. If there's a political outcry in the press about university life being too expensive for the children of poor families, Humphrey could do some research into how his fellow students finance themselves. If the headlines are talking about the problems of the increasing 'grey' population, Caroline could write about second careers or continuing to work after reaching retirement age.

Subject each of your ideas to the following tests:

- Will I be telling the readers something they don't already know?

- Is it something they'll want to know about?

- Is it topical? Does it relate to something currently uppermost in their minds?

- Will it help them to be happier, healthier, richer or better in any way?

If you can't answer 'yes' to any of these questions you probably haven't got a story and should think again.

## What Do You Want to Find Out About?

You may be quite happy to stick with the subject you're already familiar with, and I'll talk more about becoming an 'expert' in a moment. Most full-time freelance writers, however, need to have more than one subject they can write about.

So, once you've exhausted all the potential angles of your existing expertise, where will you go to next?

Humphrey the student has an almost unlimited supply of potential subject matter since he's at the beginning of his adult life and should be interested in virtually everything. He could write about career options on leaving university; travel and ways in which it can benefit young people; about drugs or music or computer games or dating or anything that concerns his peer group.

As her children grow Jackie can begin to think about where her other interests lie. Has she developed a taste for home-making? Or fashion, or food or fascism? She can follow any of them, although it'll always be easier to sell to people who've bought from her in the past. So a mother and baby magazine might be interested in a 'back to work' article from her, but she might have difficulty convincing a political editor she should write about the role of fascism in modern democracies.

All of us have something to say about the issues that affect our age group, our gender, our class or our profession. Humphrey undoubtedly has opinions about acne, dating and all-night parties, while Caroline will certainly have given some thought to the onset of middle age and men with thickening waistlines and thinning hair. Jackie will have a lot to say about school teachers, supermarkets and the commercial exploitation of Christmas, and John will know all about office politics, commuting and the burdens of being a family breadwinner. All these topics will ring bells with different target audiences and could be moulded into humorous or informative material.

There are two ways of approaching the search for new subjects. One is to follow your own interests, the other is to look what the market is hungry for and supply it. Probably you'll need to do both to generate enough work.

## Become an Expert

Anyone can become sufficiently expert in a subject to be able to write about it. Just choose the right subject and then research it. Editors, publishers and producers love experts. They have an insatiable appetite for people who sound like they know what they're talking about.

Do you already have a subject in your current profession, your hobby or something you've studied? You probably already have specialist knowledge that other people will pay for, if you can package it attractively.

Look through a few papers and magazines and note how other people are using their expertise to sell their writing work. The medical column will be written by a doctor, the gardening page by a professional gardener (probably someone you've seen on the television or heard on the radio). There'll be a cook writing about food and a career doctor advising on workplace problems.

Then there are the specialist writers who've never actually practised in the subject they write about, merely made reputations as commentators. The television critics who've never made a programme, the fashion writers who've never so much as picked up a needle and cotton or financial journalists who've never made any sort of fortune themselves. What they do have is a burning interest in the subject and knowledge of who to go to with the questions.

## Take a Long, Hard Look at the Competition

Try the following exercises.

### Exercise One

Enter a large bookshop. Walk slowly from floor to floor, drinking in the number of titles you see around you. Then say to yourself, 'This is only the tip of the iceberg. These are just the books that have come out recently or have proved themselves to be survivors. Behind them lie the invisible millions of tomes that were published and then forgotten, some within a few weeks, others after a few years.'

Do not yet draw any conclusions.

### Exercise Two

Walk to a large newsagent. Spend some time thumbing through magazines and newspapers. Then say to yourself, 'This is only the tip of the iceberg. These are just the articles that have come out in the last day, week or month. Behind them lie centuries of articles that came and went and were hardly even noticed. Also out of sight are the many magazines that don't make it on to the stands of a newsagent because their subject matter is so specialised or their potential audience so insignificant.'

Do not yet draw any conclusions.

## Exercise Three

Go home and switch on the television. (Preferably one with a few dozen satellite, cable and digital channels.) Surf the channels for an hour or two, spending no more than two or three minutes on any one programme and say to yourself, 'This is only the tip of the iceberg. Behind all these programmes are decades of archive material that was aired once and will never be seen again. Behind that lie all the pilots for all the programmes that never had their options picked up and behind them are all the scripts and treatments for programmes that no one in a position to make them ever gave a second thought to.'

Before leaving the room cast an eye over the videos and DVDs that you own and imagine the many more that are sitting in the local video store, many of them films that missed the big screen entirely.

Do not yet draw any conclusions.

## Exercise Four

Spend an hour surfing the Internet. Then say to yourself, 'This is only the tip of the iceberg. Behind this lies so many billions of words which no one beyond the writers could ever have the faintest interest in reading that it is hardly possible for me to comprehend the scale of the horror.'

The question which now must come to mind is: how on earth can any writer hope to make themselves heard among such a babble of voices? How will you ever get anyone to find the time to read what you have to say and like it enough to pay you for saying it?

Conclusion: there is good news and bad news to be gleaned from these exercises. The good news is that there is an enormous market for material out there. A lot of the products that you have spent the previous hours perusing have earned money for their authors. Someone has to provide the raw materials of the information age – why shouldn't it be you?

The British book industry alone brings out something like 125,000 new titles every year. Why shouldn't you be one of those 125,000; either this year or next year or in five years' time?

The bad news is that there just aren't enough people in the world to buy everything that's being offered, let alone have the time to read it. There are going to be books that only a few dozen people will ever read and articles that every single reader in the world will skim past on the same day. There are going to be television programmes that drift through millions of living rooms without leaving a single memory in the mind of a single viewer. That is how colossal the odds are. But you're still going to beat them.

## Ignore the Myths You Read in the Papers

We've all read of the university student who writes his or her first novel and receives a seven-figure international advance, and dreamed it might happen to us. We've also read of the writers who starved in garrets and only achieved glory after years of rejection. These are the myths of our profession. From time to time they come true, but not very often. In fact, both happen so infrequently you might as well forget about them altogether.

Even when you do read of these great sums being earned, you nearly always have to divide everything in half. The publicity and hype machines at the publishers' marketing departments are exaggerating every figure they have to catch the attention of the media. The media then double the figures again to make the story more interesting, and forget to mention tedious details such as the fact that a £1 million deal is actually spread out over ten years. 'Man gets £100,000 a year over ten years, although he'll have to pay a percentage of that to his agent and quite a lot of it is dependent on his sales figures reaching certain required levels' is not as catchy as 'Author receives £1 million for first book'.

These stories get into the papers because they're rare. They're therefore highly unlikely to happen to you or me. By all means dream about them, as you dream of the big win when you buy your lottery ticket, but don't bank on them.

## No One Else is Going to Do It for You

Another myth suggests that writers find mentors who guide them to success as surely as Colonel Tom Parker guided Elvis, or Brian Epstein the Beatles. In reality, that won't happen. Sometimes an agent or a publisher will tell you they're going to 'build your career'. Please bear in mind that most of these people are salaried employees and are quite likely to change jobs within a year and almost certainly within ten years. They'll become pregnant, have a nervous breakdown, lose their enthusiasm for the job and come up against bosses who simply don't like the work of the writers they're championing. Any agent is only on a small percentage of your earnings and will therefore have to spend most of their time looking after other clients. Likewise, any publisher has dozens of books a year to shepherd to completion. You cannot possibly be their number-one priority unless you're selling many millions of copies.

To have these people on your side is very nice indeed, but be under no illusions – your success or failure is going to be entirely dependent upon your own efforts. They may be able to help you bring your dreams to fruition, but they must be *your* dreams and *you* must be in control of their progress. You are the creator of the product, which means you are the boss. Agents are people who work for you, publishers are part financial backers, part editorial advisers, part marketing departments. Magazine editors are just customers.

If you leave your career up to any of these people it will end the moment they lose interest in you or decide to move on to something else.

# CHAPTER FOUR

# Getting Comfortable

*'The big motivation for me was the desire to be independent, to get up when you want, write what you want and work where you want.'*
Irving Wallace

That's enough doom and gloom. If I haven't managed to put you off so far, then you're probably made of stern enough stuff to survive the rigours of what is to come. Fasten your seatbelt – it's going to be a fantastic ride.

## Getting Equipped

Setting up as a freelance writer is one of the cheapest businesses possible, but there are still some pieces of equipment and services that you're going to need as surely as a window cleaner needs a bucket, mop and ladder. Spend as little money as possible at the beginning, because that's when your income will be at its lowest, but beware of false economies. Most of the new technologies have become popular because they save people time and money. A couple of thousand pounds spent well in the early stages of your career will save you a fortune later on.

Many of the things you need, like a telephone and a computer, you'll already have at home. For those who don't, these are the bare necessities.

## The Computer

There are still professional writers who don't have computers, but not many of them are under eighty. There's a little bit of the Luddite in all of us; no one likes to have to learn new skills, but some things are unavoidable.

If you do not yet have a desktop computer, start shopping around. If the shop assistants make you feel in the least bit stupid or vulnerable, don't buy anything from them yet. Instead wait until you've found one who'll be willing to field a few panic-stricken telephone calls when you get home and are unable to find the 'on' button. Don't be afraid to ask for help from friends, relatives and neighbours. Any child who's old enough to read and write can probably set you up and get you started, if you can stand to be a little patronised.

Your first priority is to have a word-processing package so that you can type, edit, store and print your work. Every computer will provide you with that.

Your next priority is to have a reasonable printer, so that you can produce professional-looking hard copies (that means printed paper) reasonably quickly.

You also need to be able to transfer your work on to computer disks, so that (a) if anything goes wrong with the machine you still have copies of your work, and (b) you can send disks to editors rather than printing up huge manuscripts.

To print out a manuscript for a book involves a ream of decent paper, an hour or so at the printer (depending on how good it is), a giant padded envelope and a small mortgage at the Post Office. When it arrives at the other end it inevitably looks dog-eared. A disk, on the other hand, costs a few pence, takes fifteen to thirty seconds to load and will travel through the post like a normal letter. At the other end the receiver can bring it straight up on to their screen and start work on it.

Many publishers now insist in their contracts on receiving the work on disk. If you send them your book in hard copy it means that someone has to retype the whole thing into another computer, which costs a fortune and takes forever, whereas with a disk the job has already been done.

Once you have a computer there are any number of other

jobs you can use it for if you're able and willing. You can keep a diary of who you've submitted work to and what their response was. You can compile your own database of contact names and addresses. You can do your accounts (see Chapter Twenty-One) and even self-publish (see Chapter Twenty-Three).

Things do sometimes go wrong with computers, such as power cuts or children interfering, so the golden rule of writing on one is: '*Always save your work onto the hard drive at regular intervals and save it onto a back-up disk at least once a day.*'

## Laptops

If you plan to travel and will be working in different locations, a laptop may be a good investment, although they are still fairly expensive. They're not crucial, because you can always carry your work around on disks and work on it on any desktop you can find. But they are a major step into the future and within a few years they'll be even cheaper and more common-place than they are today.

Since one of the great joys of being a writer is that you can work almost anywhere you want, the laptop is the obvious tool of the future. You do your research, pack your bag and head off to the beach house in Bali to do the writing. What could be better?

## Going Online

You really do need to be 'online', which means connected to the Internet. It's another large jump up the learning curve for anyone over the age of twenty who hasn't been introduced to the world of the Web (as the Internet is sometimes called) through their work, but no one who has made the jump ever wants to go back.

The most important facility the Internet offers is e-mail. With just a few keystrokes you can now send your entire manu-script down the phone line to your editor's computer within a few seconds (but only if you have their permission to do so, of course). You can be in Peru or Penzance and your editor can be in Newcastle or New York, and they will still receive it in roughly the same time and you will have paid little for the privilege, because you pay a fixed sum to your Internet service provider (ISP); even if the telephone costs are separate, you will only pay at local rates.

When you buy your computer make sure it has the capacity to go online; most do. Then ask your friends, family and work contacts about which ISP they use. Choose one that has a free helpline, just in case of teething problems. It'll take you less than one working day to get up and running and will save you hours every day from then on.

Many editors now prefer to receive all their communications via e-mail, including speculative submissions and copy.

While e-mailing is the first and most obvious reason for going online, the possibilities for research will be the next (see 'Using the Net', p.38).

## Telephones

You need to be easily contactable by telephone. Virtually every good job I've had started with a telephone enquiry. Despite the explosion in mobiles, you also need to have access to at least one landline most of the time, both for telephone calls and for access to the Internet.

A mobile phone is also useful, but it doesn't have to be more than an emergency tool if you spend most of your working time in the office or at home. If you're on your way to an appointment it's very handy to have a number on which people can reach you if they're going to be delayed or need to cancel.

Talking on a mobile in public is still a slightly uncomfortable experience for most people. You can hardly negotiate the finer points of a deal if you're sitting in a train with twenty pairs of ears listening in, or you're weaving your way through the traffic in some town centre. Nor can you interview someone with any degree of success if the line keeps breaking up.

On top of that there is the awareness at the backs of all our minds that calls on mobile phones cost a great deal more than landlines.

No doubt these inhibitions will continue to fade as the years pass and the technology improves.

## Answering Services

You need some sort of answering service. Answering machines are not expensive, but there are also services available from the telephone companies for taking messages when your line is busy. These are particularly useful if you're going to be using your normal phone line for accessing the Internet. If you're going to be online for an hour or more and an editor is trying to get through to commission an article, you must make it possible for them to leave a message, otherwise they'll call someone else.

If your work relies on fast turnaround, with daily papers asking you to provide material for deadlines a few hours away, it would probably be wise to have your computer linked to a different telephone line, so that you're more accessible. An editor who finds you're nearly always unavailable by phone and another writer isn't will start going to your rival instead of you.

## Fax Machines

Such an innovation a few years ago, fax machines now seem slightly old-fashioned, but there's still a place for them. If someone has a piece of printed material they want to get to you, then they'll often still want to fax it rather than scan it into a computer and e-mail it.

If you're going to be buying a telephone answering machine, you might as well get one that includes faxing facilities. It's always embarrassing if an editor suggests they fax something to you and you have to admit you don't have a machine. For the sake of a few extra pounds you can make yourself seem more professional. Fax machines also work as simple photocopiers. In fact, for not much more than a simple fax machine used to cost, you can buy a simple combined fax, photocopier and answering machine.

## Create a Working Womb of Your Own

To write successfully you need to be completely comfortable in whatever space you choose to set up in. It doesn't matter where it is, as long as you're happy to go there. It could be a broom cupboard under the stairs, as long as it brings you peace of mind, allowing you to forget the rest of the world exists for several hours at a time, like returning to the womb.

## Avoid the Strain

It might sound ridiculous to suggest that anyone who sits around all day staring into space, talking on the telephone or prodding at a keyboard could suffer from any physical strains, but, believe me, you can. If you spend several hours sitting in one position, repeating a limited number of movements, you'll be putting unnatural pressure on all sorts of joints and muscles, causing 'repetitive strain injury'.

The areas to watch are your back, shoulders and wrists. As soon as you can afford to buy a well-designed typing chair or stool, do so, because you'll be able to work for twice as long each day if you don't get backache. Kneeler-style seats are particularly good for posture. Make sure you take regular breaks and exercise your fingers, wrists and shoulders in different directions. If you start to develop pains in any of these areas go to an osteopath or a doctor and get it sorted out because it'll only get worse. You're going to need to spend a great many hours working in these positions if you want to be successful, so don't handicap yourself unnecessarily.

## Stationery Is Your Ambassador

Print out some decent headed notepaper. You can probably do it yourself on the computer, or will know someone who can show you how. If not, go to your local print shop. Apart from your work, this is all that some of your customers will see of you. They don't know you're sitting in a spare bedroom in your pyjamas with only a one-bar electric fire standing between you and hypothermia. If they see a professional-looking letterhead on decent-quality paper they'll make certain assumptions about how successful you are. Presentable paper and envelopes don't cost a great deal more than tatty ones. So invest a few extra pounds in making yourself look like a professional to the outside world. You'll also need compliments slips and business cards.

## Do You Need Your Own Website?

A website is probably not a necessity at the beginning, but it certainly won't do any harm and could bring in work you never even thought of going after. It's possible to set it up for yourself if you're computer-literate, or have a friend who is, and there are plenty of books on the market that will tell you what to do. It's not that expensive, however, to get a professional to help you in the early stages. It's certainly worth finding out if you can register your own name, or a close variation of it, for a website for future reference.

It's useful to be able to tell anyone who enquires about your services that they can find your CV on your website. It doesn't have to be elaborate in any way, as long as it's smart enough to convey a professional impression and offers the information that your customers need – who you are and what sort of writing you've done in the past. You can include examples of your work once you have them, lists of magazines you've contributed to and lists of subjects that you're able to write about. The potential for imaginative self-marketing is endless.

A website is a glorified advertising brochure which anyone can get access to if they just know the name, and which you can update whenever you feel like it.

Start by creating a simple 'home page' explaining who you are and where you can be contacted. You can then adapt and improve and expand the site as you become more experienced with the technology and have more to say.

If someone enquires about your services but doesn't have access to the Net you can print a copy of the site and post or fax it to them. If you're doing a mailing or any sort you can include the same material, updating it as you go along.

Any CV needs to have only the barest of facts. Potential

clients do not need to know any personal information about you, or what schools you went to, although if you're writing about a profession you've worked in and are now writing about, it might be useful to mention any relevant degrees or professional qualifications. The most important thing is to mention what you've written, where it was published and the subjects you specialise in. Don't pad it out with any flowery descriptions; keep it short and factual. All prospective clients want to know is (a) can you write? and (b) do you know anything about the subject they're looking for?

## Recording Equipment

If you're going to be interviewing you'll need a small, portable cassette recorder. Choose one that is as discreet and simple as possible. A small cassette player, with a built-in microphone, that can stand on a table near them will soon be forgotten about. Make sure you change the batteries long before they're likely to run out. Nothing could be more annoying than doing a brilliant interview only to find that your recorder didn't pick up a single word. (See also 'Doing Interviews', p.74.)

You may need a larger desktop machine to play the cassettes back on as sound quality on portable machines can sometimes be poor. There are more expensive machines on the market, which you can upgrade to once you know what your requirements will be.

## Shorthand Skills

Many professional news reporters still use traditional shorthand for recording interviews and it would certainly be useful to learn the skill if you have the time – a sort of 'belt and braces' approach to interviewing. There'll be times when it's impossible to use a recorder because of background noise or because of the subject's voice. It would then be very helpful to be able to jot down what they were saying and be confident you would be able to read it back once you got back to the safety of your working womb.

So, are you sitting comfortably? Then we'll begin.

# CHAPTER FIVE

# Selling Your Ideas

*'You have to get lucky at some point, but you can only get lucky if you are still on the road, and for each of us that road, that journey, is of a different length. The thing is to keep doing it and doing it, any way you can.'*
Lawrence Kasdan

In this chapter I will suggest tactics for selling your work to customers such as book publishers and magazine editors. In the following chapter I will look at the broader subject of creating a strategic marketing campaign for yourself. You need to bear both concepts in mind from day one. Some of the information is relevant to both chapters; for example, the section on 'Direct Mail' in Chapter Six (see p.63) is also relevant to selling your ideas.

## Welcome to the Casino

Imagine walking into a casino. Instead of having pockets full of money to gamble on the tables you have your manuscript. You don't have any idea whether you'll be leaving the casino empty-handed or with a £1-million publishing contract and a promise from Steven Spielberg to turn your brainchild into his next mega-blockbuster.

The odds are nearly always against you, particularly at the beginning of your career when no one knows who you are and you have no track record, but the possibility of winning is what will keep you going back.

Occasionally the casino will produce a jackpot. J.K. Rowling was rejected by the first agent she approached, but the second accepted her, which meant she was quickly in the game. After that the first few numbers she put her bet on came up with nothing – in other words she was turned down by the first few publishers who saw the work – then she hit the number which opened the vaults and produced a National Lottery-sized win. The odds against that happening were phenomenal, and for every J.K. Rowling there are thousands of people who pick losing numbers and leave the table disappointed, but if you don't join the game it's absolutely certain you won't ever have a chance at the jackpot, whereas if you do there will always be little wins along the way to keep you going.

But surely, I hear you cry, gambling is a mug's game, and you're right. But in this case you aren't gambling with money – because that is a mug's game – you're merely gambling with your time and energy. Anyone who works in a speculative industry is doing that. We all run the risk of failing, but join the game because you never know, today may be your lucky day, and if it isn't, there's always tomorrow.

## Who Are Your Potential Customers?

You have to identify your potential customers. For articles, start with the media you consume yourself. If you're a regular reader of a particular newspaper or magazine, the chances are you'll want to write for it, since it shares your general view on life.

Now start to investigate all the media you haven't yet come across and, believe me, you'll only ever have seen the tip of the iceberg.

## Reference Books

Go to a bookshop's reference section and look for writer's guides with names and addresses of literary agents, publishers and magazine editors and film and television programme makers.

Next go to the local library and ask for the sort of media

guides used by the advertising and public relations industries. These will list publications that you'll never see on the shelves of your local newsagents. Whether your line of expertise is breeding caged birds, building model cathedrals with match-sticks or combating international terrorism, the chances are there are several magazines for enthusiasts of the subject which are constantly on the lookout for new material.

There are editorial guides in existence that list all the person-nel on major or local newspapers, from business editors to sports editors to pig-farming correspondents. They're constantly being updated and are therefore expensive to buy, so, unless you have a friend in the advertising industry who can pass on old ones, you'll need to look at them in a library.

## Build Your List

Then there are the magazines and newspapers themselves. Study the editorial page and see if it lists the editors or the commissioning editors. Keep a list of potential contacts, with descriptions of the sort of material they're likely to buy, and update it all the time. Unfortunately, people change jobs so often that it's impossible to have a finite list, but you can at least build up a network of leads, telephone numbers and e-mail addresses which you can use when you have something specific to market.

If it's a book you're hoping to sell, look round your local bookshop and find similar titles, making a note of which publishers seem to specialise in that field. Then find the address and telephone number of those publishers in a refer-ence book – or ring directory enquiries.

Before you send anything off into the blue (and I'll discuss what you should send later), whether it's to a publishing editor or a television producer, phone up and see if they'll give you an appropriate name to address it to. Be ready to explain what it is you want to send if they answer the phone themselves and ask you about your project. Unless they ask you to tell them, however, you should stick to requesting their details so that you can send them something. If someone feels cornered on the telephone they'll play safe and say 'no'; if they get it in writing they're less likely to make a hasty decision, which increases the chances that you'll get a positive answer.

It's much more effective to address a letter to an individual rather than a job title; to 'Fred Bloggs, Editorial Director' rather than simply 'Editorial Director'. Some companies won't give out the names of staff members, in which case you need to ask them what the right job title is. They may have people whose sole job it is to sift through unsolicited material; everything has to go through them and if you can establish some sort of personal contact you're already ahead of the game.

## Using the Net

If you don't want to venture out of the house in your search for customers, then there's always the Internet. Virtually every piece of information you could need is out there in cyberspace somewhere; you just need to find a way of tracking it down. The best way to become skilful on the Net is trial and error. Just keep typing in keywords you think will trigger the sort of information you need. If, for instance, you want to know more about a book publisher who you think might be interested in your manuscript, look at their website first. This may give you specific instructions about what to do next, but if it doesn't it will still give you a good idea of the sort of material they're looking for; the same with magazines.

Many of the major libraries and reference works are also on the Internet now. It's always easy to become impatient with the Net; you spend half an hour trying to find one piece of information and become so frustrated you give up, deciding that modern technology isn't all it's cracked up to be. Consider the alternatives for a moment. A trip to a bricks-and-mortar library will probably involve you in driving into town, maybe paying for a car park, finding the right book (which the library may not have, in which case you've wasted several hours). You then either take it home (which will involve another trip to return it), or sit down with a pencil and paper and copy out addresses, or wrestle with a coin-operated photocopier. Working on screen, however, you have no travelling time or costs and you can print anything you want at the press of a button. However frustrating technology may be, most of the time it isn't half as frustrating as the real world.

## Just a Keystroke Away

Virtually every potential customer is working at a screen at some time of the day and is therefore connected to an e-mail address and can be contacted either directly or through an assistant or a secretary. Getting direct e-mail addresses is sometimes as hard as getting direct telephone numbers, but not always. Some people are quite happy to hear from strangers in this way. So start building a list of potential customers and their e-mail addresses.

It's not a good idea to send unsolicited e-mails of more than a few lines. People do not want to spend time downloading massive attachments unless they know what they are. They do not want their lines blocked with unsolicited 1000-page manuscripts. Always observe the etiquette of treating others as you would like to be treated yourself. First e-mail them a short note asking for permission to send something longer.

## Now Leave Them Alone

Build a potential customer list, which includes everyone who might possibly be interested in the idea or piece you are intending to sell. But do not waste their time with inappropriate material. Only contact them when you're clear in your mind what you're going to be offering them, because once you've had an idea rejected you can't go back with it again, at least not for a year or two. So keep your contacts ready for when you have a sure-fire offer to make to them.

## Put Yourself in Their Shoes

Salespeople are taught to put themselves in their customers' shoes to work out what they need and want, and then to offer it to them. The same principle will work for you. Let's look at your potential customers.

## The Book Publisher

In her novel *Bestseller* Olivia Goldsmith says, 'As difficult as it is for a writer to find a publisher – admittedly a daunting task – it is twice as difficult for a publisher to sort through the chaff, select the wheat, and profitably publish a worthy list.'

The commissioning editor in a publishing house, who is the person you will be selling your ideas to, is almost certainly overworked and underpaid. As well as buying and editing books, they also have to attend meetings, produce paperwork and manage their projects. The last thing you should do is add to their burden. What they want are book projects that will involve them in as little work as possible, will be easy to market and will impress their bosses. They will also want to pay as little as possible for them. It's only with the last of these wishes that you need to fight, but with all the others you should help in any way you can.

What editors do not want is a huge manuscript they have to plough all the way through before they can decide whether or not to buy it. Nor do they want something so badly written they're going to have to spend weeks editing or rewriting. Nor do they want to commission something that might not be as good as promised or won't turn up by the date it's due.

They are not waiting to be offered some wonderful new piece of work. More often they're deciding the sort of things they want to publish first and going out to find writers who can meet their needs. That gives them even less time to spend on any ideas you might send in on spec.

Above all else, aim to save the editor as much time as possible. This rule needs to be borne in mind at all times.

## The Magazine or Newspaper Editor

Every day, week or month (depending on the frequency with which they publish), magazine and newspaper editors have to find enough stories to fill enough pages to balance out the advertising their publications carry. To make a profit they have to find material that will appeal to as many potential readers as possible, and buy it before their rivals. Whereas a book editor might have six months from the moment an author submits a manuscript until they publish, the editor of a daily newspaper has to find a similar number of words by the late afternoon every day. A single edition of a broadsheet newspaper may contain 70,000 words.

The pressures therefore are different. There is more of a rush, but there is also more money available to pay for anything that fits their needs.

The golden rule, however, remains the same. The commodity they're shortest of is time. If you can save any of that for them, then you will immediately have them on your side.

Always have a synopsis of your article available, no more than a few dozen words long, which will spell out the main points, so that you can read it to prospective customers over the phone, or send it if they show some interest but want to know more before committing themselves.

## The Television and Film Producer

The pressures are different again in television and film (see Chapter Seventeen). A major film producer might only be thinking about one film for months on end. While they may well be looking at other things during that period, they will not be giving the hunt for material their full attention. That makes the job of catching their eye a great deal harder, because there are only certain times when they will be receptive to new ideas.

In the television companies that produce steady streams of projects along similar lines – situation comedies perhaps, or game shows – there will be people continually assessing new ideas. In those cases the golden rules change. They probably have time to read most of the well-presented material that finds its way to them, as long as it's both relevant to their needs and sufficiently different to catch their attention – not an easy brief for a writer to fill.

## How to Sell a Book

You need to provide enough material to demonstrate to the commissioning editor that the eventual book will be substantial and filled with good things, and you need to sell it succinctly so that it doesn't take potential customers too long to read it and to be enthused.

The concept will have to be sold many times over. You may convince the editor that the project deserves a decent advance, but that editor has then got to persuade his or her financial and marketing people to agree. These are busy people who do not have the time (or, in many cases, the inclination) to spend much of their time reading. So you need to spell out, right at the beginning of the document, why they should be reading it, to either coax them into reading further, or convince them they can make an offer without going further than the first page.

The more material you're willing to produce on spec, the happier the commissioning editor will be, but you have to balance the need to prove that the book is a potential winner against your own need to earn a living. You probably can't afford to spend a couple of months putting together a synopsis when there's always a chance that no one will make an offer for it. Most synopses, of course, won't take anything like that long.

There will be the odd case where the material is so commercial you'll only have to provide a page or two for publishers to be falling over themselves to make an offer, but those sorts of stories are few and far between. In most cases you'll have to do most of the following:

- Write a basic synopsis of a few thousand words which explains the whole story, where the material will come from and why it will attract readers. List other books that have tapped into the same market and explain why this one will be better and different. You can get this information from your local bookshop or one of the online bookstores. (If there are too many titles in the sector and you don't have anything radically new to offer, then you'll know you're barking up the wrong tree.) If there is any captive market, find out how large that market is and put the statistics into the synopsis. For example, if it's a book about golf, find out how many people in Britain play golf and how much they spend on the game, and explain why your book would appeal to them. If your book is likely to become required reading at universities or colleges around the world or a set text in schools, the prospective publisher will be able to make a good prediction of the numbers that will be sold.

- Distil everything you've said in the synopsis down to 100–200 words, making it as punchy as it will be when it appears on the back of the final book. That will be the first page of the synopsis.

- Distil it down even more to a one- or two-line explanation of the kind you might find in a publisher's catalogue, or as you might describe the book to someone at a cocktail party. That will give you your opening lines.

- Write 100–200 words about yourself as the author. This doesn't have to have every detail of your educational, personal and employment history, but just the points that the publisher could use to promote you and your work. They want to know why you're the best person to write this particular book. If you have any credentials in the subject matter of the book, boast about them. They want to know that you're at least a 'leading expert' and preferably the best in the business. They also want to know how they might be able to interest journalists in interviewing you once the book has come out. There's no harm in creating some sort of writer's myth around yourself.

- Provide a chapter breakdown. You don't have to feel you're casting the book in concrete, as no one will remember what you promised to put in each chapter when you finally hand the manuscript in several months down the line, but they need to see roughly how the book will be structured. It'll help to reassure them that the subject will stretch out to a whole book. You could make the chapter breakdown work as the main synopsis, particularly if the material runs chronologically.

- You may also need to write a sample chapter. This should probably be the opening chapter, because then you can pull out all the stops to make it as gripping as you can, so they can't wait to read the rest.

## How to Sell an Article

Once you've compiled a list of subjects you know about, write some articles. (It's probably better to start with articles and move on later to books and scripts, simply because articles are shorter and easier to sell.) Try writing 1000 words on each subject, and then prepare another draft on the same subject at 500 words. It's possible you'll want to discard your first few attempts and try again. Don't worry; it's all part of the apprenticeship. If you were setting out on a career in furniture-making you would probably not be able to sell your first few efforts.

Don't send the whole article off at first. Distil it down to a sentence or two, including something to sell you as the author. For example:

- 'I'm a student and I've been researching an article into the ten best methods of financing a gap year abroad. I've compared the pros and cons of the five most popular destinations.'

- 'I'm a mother of three and have compiled a light-hearted but practical article about what can go wrong at children's parties and how to avoid the many pitfalls.'

- 'As a professional financial adviser I'm often asked by clients about the advantages and disadvantages of buying a property to rent. To meet this need I've written a 1000-word article on the subject, answering all the most commonly asked questions.'

- 'In my career as a qualified personnel director, I've frequently been shocked by how often companies take on people who are obviously completely unsuited to their corporate environment. As a result I've written a 1000-word guide on how to fit the right person to the right job.'

Then write or e-mail your contacts and ask them if they would like to see the piece. If they always publish articles of 500 words, don't offer them anything longer. Match what you offer as closely as possible to what you know about their needs.

At this stage you're selling the ideas rather than the actual articles. Concentrate on making them as interesting and to the point as possible. Once an editor has bought the ideas, you can then worry about selling them the article itself and your writing style.

## Keep Records

Always keep a record of who you send what to and when. You'll be surprised how quickly the rejections and re-submissions start piling up, and if you're sending out half a dozen different ideas in rotation to a list or twenty or thirty editors, it won't be long before you lose track of who's seen what. Don't send them the same angle twice, and follow up with a phone call or e-mail if you haven't received a response. A week after sending the idea, ask politely if they've received it and if they'd be interested in seeing the article when it's written. It's possible they'll have forgotten all about your approach and you'll have to remind them of what it said. If you're talking over the phone they'll probably make a decision on the spot.

Once you've sold a few articles to an editor, and built up the relationship to a point where they recognise your name when you call, you can begin to suggest ideas over the phone and cut out the initial approach. This will speed up the process considerably, allowing you to find out within minutes if an idea is a goer. Before you make the call, however, write down what the article will be about, with the main selling points, so that you can put the case swiftly and succinctly and not waste their time with waffle.

If an editor says 'no', accept it as final. You could, however, just ask if there is anything else you could do for them. If they say 'no' again, leave them alone until you have another idea to offer them.

The moment you have a 'no' you can send the idea off to the next person on the list, and try to think of something else to offer the editor who's just turned you down. The objective is constantly to remind them of your existence and of your willingness to do whatever they need, but not to pester them.

While you're continuing this hunt for customers, you should

be writing the articles anyway. There are a number of reasons for doing this.

- You need the experience and the practice.

- You need the information in order to sound authoritative when selling the idea.

- While doing the research you may stumble across other angles and ideas you could be selling at the same time.

- An editor might say 'yes' but demand to see the article immediately. You need to be prepared.

- Once you've written something you'll have a definite product to sell rather than just an idea for one.

## When an Editor Says 'Yes'

An editor has said 'yes' to one of your ideas. But what sort of 'yes' is it? They may be saying, 'Yes, the idea is good. We're willing to look at the article if you'd like to send it.' They may still reject it, but at least you're one step further on.

Alternatively, they may be saying, 'Yes, we'll commission the article.' In that case you need to know the following:

- How many words they want.

- What the deadline is.

- How much they're going to pay and what they want you to do about pictures. (Do they want you to take photographs and charge them or ask people if they have library shots or portraits of themselves?)

Without making them think you don't know how to approach the subject, ask if there are any angles they particularly want covered and anyone they would especially like you to quote in the article. The more closely you tailor the piece to their requirements, the more likely they are to use you again. You also need as many leads as possible to make the piece as thorough as you can. Again, make sure you have fully understood which kind of 'yes' it is. If you're not sure and don't want to ask, assume it's the first kind until you've received a formal acceptance.

Some editors might send you an official commissioning letter – but not many will have the time – and if asked I'd suggest you say you don't need one. You do, after all, need to build up a relationship of mutual trust with these people. Occasionally they'll let you down, but not very often.

If you think a misunderstanding could arise at a later date, drop them a confirming note outlining what you've agreed to do, when they can expect to receive it and how much the agreed fee is.

Make sure you have a copy of the magazine you're writing for. If you can meet the editor personally, so much the better for the sake of building up a long-term relationship. If they don't have time to see you, don't insist. Equally, if they're based at the other end of the country or overseas, a visit would be impractical.

Read the magazine carefully to see what sort of style they like. Do they use a lot of quotes? Do they like long sentences and paragraphs, or do they like everything short and snappy? Do they assume a certain level of knowledge in their readers, or do they explain everything in detail?

Each sort of publication is different. A broadsheet newspaper has a very different style to a tabloid, for example, and most newspapers and magazines have their own way of talking to their readers. You won't be able to get it exactly right for all of them, but they'll expect you to get reasonably close, so that they can edit and adjust what you've done without too much effort.

The more trouble you take at this stage, the more likely you'll get it right first time. This will not only save you time on rewriting, but will also make them keener to use you again.

If, once you start researching, it turns out there isn't a story there, admit it straight away rather than trying to fob the editor off with something half-baked. Explain why you don't think you're going to be able to deliver, and ask if they have any ideas on how you can overcome the problem. Most editors will do their best to be helpful if they feel you're being honest with them.

## Will They Pay You?

In the early stages you may not always be paid for your work. You should try to get a fee wherever you can, but sometimes it's more important to get an article published, so that you have something to show the next potential customer, than getting the money.

If an editor likes the ideas you've pitched to them, they will probably ask to see the piece. Ask what their deadline is and stick to it. Show them you're completely professional and reliable.

They may offer you a fee before they see it, but they may not. If they don't, then ask them how much they pay. They'll have standard rates, which they'll tell you, although they may make it clear they'll only pay if they like what you write.

Once you've sent in the article and they've said they like it, ask if you can invoice for it at the rate they suggested. They'll probably agree, although they may say they'll only pay upon publication. Ask them when publication is likely to be. If they then don't publish it, ring again and ask if they intend to use the article, or whether you can try to sell it to someone else. At that stage, if they still want it, they'll probably offer to pay you for it rather than lose it to a rival. If they don't offer to pay at this stage they're probably not that interested and you'd be well advised to send the piece to someone else.

Some people, like certain professional writers' associations and unions, will tell you there are minimum rates of pay below which you shouldn't go. They'll also say you should have formal commissioning letters, and that the editors should agree to pay a rejection fee if they end up not using the article.

If you start insisting on all that, I'm afraid you're not going to get much further. At this stage in your career you need the editors far more than they need you. They'll have a standard rate for the job, and, I must repeat, when you're starting out it's more important to get your work published than to get paid.

If you mention a rejection fee the editor will think you're unsure you can come up with the goods. Assume they're going to love whatever you send them. If, for any reason, they don't, it's probably because you haven't done it well enough.

Remember that if you do a good job and they don't use the article, you can sell it to a rival title later on.

You can, however, ask if they'd be prepared to pay expenses on top of the fee. This doesn't mean the cost of minor items like paper and disks, but could include travel expenses, large telephone bills and so on. If they say 'no', don't pursue it.

If they reject the piece for any reason, don't argue. You'll never change their minds but just annoy them and make them less inclined to take your calls in the future.

Once the piece has been published you can invoice and start chasing the money just as you would for any other service.

As you become more experienced this will all change. You'll get to know who pays what and which editors are true to their word and which will mess you about. Eventually, once they know you're reliable, they'll be ringing you and commissioning pieces, in which case they'll have to tell you the fee in advance.

At this stage, concentrate on getting published, establishing good contacts and building your portfolio. Better to have an article published in a university magazine or local paper, which you can then put on your website and add to your printed CV than to have a list of rejections from the *Financial Times* and *Vanity Fair*.

## Handling Rejection

The author Alex Haley said wisely, 'Beginning writers must appreciate the prerequisites if they hope to become writers. You pay your dues – which takes years.' I cannot overstate the need to be thick-skinned and philosophical in the face of the knock-backs you're going to receive. If you approach them with the right attitude, it'll be water off a duck's back.

Anyone too sensitive to handle rejection is doomed. But how do you learn to cope? The first thing to take on board is that when an editor turns down work you've sent in on spec the rejection isn't personal. It seems personal because your idea feels like your baby, like a part of yourself. It may also feel personal because at school you were taught that there are right and wrong answers to everything. If you got a C– for an essay and your best friend got an A+, then you must, in some way, have done worse than your friend. What you didn't know at the time was that the teacher's judgement was totally subjective. With another teacher your essay might be the one with the A+ and your friend might be the one being crushed by the C–.

If an editor rejects your work you may well assume it isn't good enough. It's possible you're right. It's also possible that it isn't what that editor wants, but it may be exactly what another one wants. Many times I have sent out a piece of work to more than one editor and received contradictory responses. One editor might say the piece was too descriptive and didn't bring out the character of the protagonists clearly enough, while the other might praise the characters but decline to buy it because there wasn't enough description. You only have to read a few reviews of books in different newspapers to see that one man's meat is another's fish and yet another's worst nightmare.

Say to yourself, regularly: *'I will never please everyone, but I must keep searching for the ones I can please.'*

## What a Publisher's Rejection Slip Really Means

The standard rejection slip from a book publisher will seldom give you a true idea of why your work is being rejected. If it's a printed form it'll say something to the effect that your work doesn't fit in with their needs at that moment. That may be partly true. It may also be true that:

- They've spent their budget for the year and have nothing left for you.

- They're already working seven days a week and don't even have time to read your manuscript, let alone work with you on it.

- They hate the sort of thing you write.

- They hate this particular piece of work.

- They don't know how they would sell the book if they did publish it.

■ The commissioning editor is planning to leave the job in a few weeks and once they're at their new publishing house they'll be ringing you and offering you tens of thousands of pounds for your brilliant work. (Only kidding, but it's a nice dream all the same.)

## Rejection by Other Mediums

If a magazine or newspaper is rejecting something you've sent them they'll probably just ignore you, unless you already have a personal relationship with the editor. They haven't rung you because they have a thousand other things to think about and ringing to tell someone they're not going to be buying their article is not a job anyone wants. They'll be hoping they never hear from you again. We'll talk about what you should do in that situation later, but suffice it to say that the one thing you shouldn't feel is insulted. They've probably already commissioned or recently run a similar feature or they know it wouldn't be of interest to their particular readership. Thank them kindly for their trouble and promise to come back with something better next time.

In the film and television world rejection is even less personal because the odds against success are even higher. To publish a book costs a publisher anything from £10,000 to many times that amount. To finance a feature film can cost tens of millions, so very few get made. One book will, at the most, take up a few months of an editor's time, while a feature film will keep producers and directors in a state of near panic for years. Despite the odds, there are still countless people sending in scripts and treatments that are absolutely bound to be rejected because no one will be able to raise sufficient money.

If this is the field you want to work in you'll have to accept that it's the table in the casino where only the highest rollers can prosper. You'll always be allowed to pull up a chair, but most of the time you'll lose. When you do win, however, you win very big money indeed. You also need to accept the possibility that your number may never, ever come up, and have another string to your bow just to ensure that you don't starve to death while you're waiting for your luck to change.

It's very hard, when you're not all that confident about whether you can be a writer at all, to be told that something over which you've lavished hours, days or even weeks of loving care and attention is 'not quite what we're looking for'. When it happens there's a strong temptation to argue. *Don't!* They are the customers and you have to give them what they want. If they aren't satisfied you must try again.

Alternatively, there may be a temptation to give up and slink away to lick your wounds in private. *Don't.* You can't become a professional writer unless you can withstand this sort of thing.

If they're being very friendly and don't seem to want to get rid of you as quickly as possible, try asking them to explain why it's wrong, and do everything you can to put it right. You'll always learn something from any criticism – much more, in fact, than if they say nothing and rewrite the article themselves. Going that way might save you time and bother, but it'll teach you nothing and will not encourage editors to use you again. Show how eager you are to learn, and ask them to tell you where you're going wrong. If you have received an impersonal rejection do not annoy the sender by going back and asking for reasons.

The best way to handle rejection is to have so many projects on the go at any one time that you always have something to be optimistic about. If you complete an article, send it out and then sit back and wait to have it accepted you're almost bound to be disappointed. If you forget about it the moment you finish it, immediately turning your attention to something new, you won't feel so bruised when the first rejections come in.

Think of it this way: if you aren't getting rejections then you aren't being ambitious enough. Only people who stick their necks out get rejected, people who play safe and never do anything difficult, never fail.

There are thousands of stories of books that were rejected by publishers and went on to sell millions. A book I ghostwrote called *Sold* was rejected by every publisher in London bar one and went on to sell over three million copies. But the story to bear in mind when you're feeling particularly low is that of

James Lee Burke. His *The Lost Get-Back Boogie* is reputed to have been rejected 111 times before finding a home and then went on to be nominated for the Pulitzer Prize.

Remember the one golden rule above all others, the one that you must chant to yourself as you go to sleep each night: '*I must never, never, never give up trying.*'

## Why Publishers Don't Know Any More Than You Do

Publishers actually have no more idea what will work than you do. All they know is what has and hasn't worked in the past; they have no way of knowing whether similar projects will work in the future.

No one can ever predict which books will be runaway bestsellers. All they can do is see a way in which they can recover their costs as fast as possible and bring the book to the attention of the general public. They need to be able to see who they would market it to, and they'll feel more comfortable if they know of other books that have trodden a similar path to success in the past.

If there's a celebrity name or some controversial material involved they'll be even more comfortable because they'll know they'll have at least a reasonable chance of publicity. Publishers, however, are aware they need to pay advances (see 'Approaching the Publisher for an Advance', p.100) if they're going to get the books with the best chance of success, and, if you package it effectively, yours will be one of them.

## You Can't Have Too Much Work

Never turn work down because you don't think you'll have time to do it – there's always time. Only turn it down because it isn't financially viable or because you don't want to do it. If you turn an editor down once they may never come back to you again.

There have been times when I've been working on half a dozen books simultaneously, and doing articles and business writing on the side, and I've felt strongly tempted to panic and try to get out of some of the projects. Experience has taught me, however, that out of five major projects, one will be cancelled, two will be delayed and the remaining two will prove to be easier than you expected.

Even so, you should always let your customers know the situation. Explain that you have other things on – they'll appreciate the fact that you're in demand – and give them sensible dates by which you can deliver the work. If it has to be pushed through, see if any of your other projects are running ahead of schedule and can be interrupted to allow a rush job.

It sometimes helps, in the middle of a large project like a book, to take a break for a week or two to do something completely different. You can then return to the job, which might have been becoming something of a burden, refreshed and full of new enthusiasm.

## Will They Steal My Idea?

Yes, they might, but they probably won't. I often meet would-be writers who've never sent their ideas to anyone for fear they'll be stolen. By doing that they not only safeguard themselves against theft, but they also guarantee themselves against success. Life is risky and sometimes you get your fingers burned. Anyone who goes into the casino runs the risk of losing their money, being cheated by other players or mugged on the way home with their winnings. Would it be more sensible to stay outside in the parking lot? I don't think so.

Keep a copy of all work you do, and maybe a copy of any letter or e-mail you send out with a submission. That way you will, if push comes to shove, be able to prove in a court of law that you had the idea first and, if the thief has been successful, you'll reap the rewards of a handsome pay-out just to get you off their backs. I met an author who'd written a children's book that had been a quite respectable success and had then drifted into the obscurity that awaits most books. A few years later one of the biggest films in the world came out bearing an uncanny resemblance to his book. The amount of money the company was likely to pay him in damages far exceeded anything even the most optimistic agent would have asked for if they had come to him to buy the rights at the beginning, when nobody knew what a success the film would be.

Never be bitter but always try to get a fair deal. Don't waste money on lawyers unless there's a very good chance indeed of success on a major scale, because they will drain your pockets and your energies, leaving you entirely unable to write anything else.

# CHAPTER SIX

# Be Your Own Marketing Guru

*'A ratio of failure is built into the process of writing. The wastepaper basket has evolved for a reason.'*
Margaret Atwood

The previous chapter was about selling specific project ideas. This is about marketing you as a provider of writing services, so that (a) people will come to you to commission work, and (b) when you go to them with ideas they'll know who you are and be keen to buy from you.

## Polishing Your Corporate Image

People feel more comfortable buying from companies that look competent and prosperous. The same applies to individuals who want to sell us something. We all judge by appearances, however much we might tell ourselves we shouldn't. Writers are allowed a little more eccentricity in their appearance and behaviour than most professionals, but it still helps to cultivate an air of efficiency and self-confidence. It starts with the presentation of your work. I've already talked about the importance of good notepaper and calling cards, and a reliable computer and printer. It's not a good idea to reuse envelopes and fasten them with layers of Sellotape, which will make it impossible to open them easily. Think of the impression your submission letter or manuscript will make when it's opened. Do you want the recipient to think you're some sad old bloke in a bedsit, or a successful professional who makes a good enough living to be able to afford decent stationery?

The same applies to your personal appearance. You do not have to dress in Versace or arrive for an editorial meeting in a Ferrari, but you do have to put prospective clients at their ease. In some cases it might pay to be flamboyant. If you're on a book tour and you want to get your picture in the papers, then it wouldn't hurt to put a little show business into your act. After all, Tom Wolfe has his white suits and Noel Coward had an unmistakable image, as does Jackie Collins and as did Barbara Cartland.

When you visit clients they need to feel you're capable of doing the job and, if it's a book you're writing, that you'll have the presence to promote it once it's published. Dress accordingly.

If you're going to interview people and research your material, you need to allow others to shine. You're there to be the observer, not the observed. You do not need to turn up looking like Oscar Wilde or Joan Collins. Any obvious dressing up or dressing down will be counterproductive. Modesty and invisibility are what you should be striving for, so that they will not give your appearance a second thought.

If you go to see a doctor or a solicitor and they're wearing a suit of a reasonably conservative cut, or casual but clean clothes, you'll feel quite happy about trusting them with your medical or legal problems. That is the same effect that you need to instil in your interviewees.

## Letting the Consumer Media Know You Exist

You need to let editors and producers know you're an expert in your field and would like to contribute articles or regular columns to their magazines and papers, or appear in a regular slot on their radio or television shows.

You need to give them a brief résumé of your professional qualifications and then a list of suggested subjects. When you start out you should approach everyone, from your local papers to the nationals, from local radio stations to television magazine programmes.

If you've already had some articles published in your trade press that will help to give you credibility as an expert, but you'll have to adjust the subject matter to suit a more general audience. The office furniture expert, for instance, will have to talk about the back problems caused by the wrong types of chair, or the dangers of using computers on unsuitable tables and desks, or the health hazards of air conditioning in offices. Alternatively, they might be able to make predictions about the office of the future that will catch the imagination of editors and producers.

Once you have a reputation as having specialist knowledge in a subject, editors will be constantly approaching you to give opinions on anything even vaguely related to the subject. They need to quote you in other articles, which won't earn you any money but will feed your reputation, and they'll want you to write your own thoughts down for them. If you're an expert on guns or explosives your phone will be red-hot whenever a shooting makes the front page or a war seems imminent. If your specialist subject is shopping, then any rumours that a major supermarket is going out of business or overcharging or giving their customers food poisoning will have the editors beating a path to your door for comments. Financial experts are continually being wheeled out to try to explain to the rest of us what is happening in the markets.

For this to happen, however, you'll have to make sure that they know of your existence and they know how to contact you at short notice.

## Offer Choices and Ask Customers What They Want

When you're offering ideas for articles to an editor, be ready to accept whatever they want. If an editor does ask you to do something and it's humanly possible, then you must do it. You have to build relationships with people who are in a position to give you repeat business.

Once you've sold them one article you can offer them lists of possible ideas to choose from and, whenever you're talking to them, ask if there's anything else you could help them with. Imagine you're running a high-class fruit and vegetable stall. A customer buys an apple for their lunch. If you have the time you'll show them a few of the best things on the stall in the hope of tempting them and end by asking, 'Anything else for you today?' If you don't ask the question it's quite likely they'll wander off with their apple without another thought. If you do ask them they just might remember they've got someone coming to lunch the next day and will need to put together a salad.

## Get Yourself Noticed

I've stressed that in general writers need to make themselves presentable but inconspicuous. But there's always an exception to the rule, and if you're going to be a leading expert in your subject it doesn't hurt to make yourself look a little different. A television gardener who doesn't wear a bra or an interior designer who dresses like an eighteenth-century dandy are more likely to imprint themselves on the memories of the media and the public than their greyer colleagues. Chefs who talk with cockney accents or swear at their staff, wine experts who make ridiculous extravagant claims for the flavours they can taste, astronomers with monocles and racing tipsters in deerstalkers, all add to the gaiety of the nation and by giving themselves distinctive trademarks they increase their celebrity status and consequently the saleability of their written work.

If you're a good writer, becoming a celebrity will always help you to sell your work in other areas for better prices. Alan Titchmarsh is mainly famous for his gardening skills, but when he turned his hand to fiction-writing his agent was able to get him some very healthy advances from publishers who might have been a great deal harder to persuade had he still been an occasional daytime television presenter. Jamie Oliver, Nigella Lawson and Delia Smith can sell their cookery books by the truckload because they're recognisable names. You don't have to be famous to get a generous upfront payment (see 'Approaching the Publisher for an Advance', p.100), but it certainly doesn't hurt. In a market as crowded as publishing, everyone wants to have a recognisable name attached to a project and will be willing to pay a premium to get one. You could be that celebrity.

## Be Led by the Marketplace

It may be that you'll become an expert by default. At one stage I was given a lot of work by a marketing magazine. This encouraged me to go to other general business publications and claim, with a little justification, that I was 'a marketing writer'. If you can persuade an editor to accept a few articles on a subject that is dear to your heart, it won't be long before you can market yourself as an expert in that subject. The truth is, anyone can become an expert, simply by finding out the answers to problems and passing them on to others.

Very early in my career I was commissioned to write the history of one of the London drama schools. In the process of meeting teachers and pupils from its past I started to learn about the history of the other schools as well. By the time I'd finished the book I was confident enough of the subject to approach magazines as 'an expert' on the subject and went to the other leading schools to do more interviews and research. As a result I was able to place articles in a dozen or so places, including prestigious titles like *Illustrated London News* and *Country Life*, which I could then package up and send to other publications as examples of my work.

## You Are a Service Provider

You're not just selling a product. You're also selling a service. A garage may be primarily there to keep your car working for you. If, however, you have a choice between two different garages, one of which is clean and tidy and always turns your car round in a day, while the other is a filthy oily mess, never completes a job on time and frequently overcharges, there's no question which establishment you will decide to frequent.

You're working in just as competitive a marketplace as any garage owner. If a newspaper or magazine editor rings you up and you're always irritable, he'll start ringing someone else. If you're always telling him you're under pressure and can't meet his deadlines, he's going to start ringing someone else. If you promise to deliver on time and then let him down, he'll ring someone else next time. Likewise, if you turn in work that needs a lot of editing, he'll turn to someone else.

An editor will take it for granted that a professional freelance writer can write. He will be buying you on the strength of the service you offer, which means helping him with ideas, meeting deadlines, doing extra work if required without complaining and generally making his life as pleasant as possible.

That doesn't mean you have to go over the top and send flowers on his birthday, but he'll be impressed if you offer to pay for lunch occasionally when you're going to be meeting anyway. (Don't try to browbeat an editor into lunch if he's at all reluctant. It may be that he doesn't have time and will resent spending two hours in the middle of the working day with someone who's trying to sell themselves to him.)

## Building Relationships with Customers

In any selling situation the first sale is always the hardest. The customer doesn't know who you are, how good you are or how reliable. They're taking a leap of faith in commissioning anything from you. Once you've delivered the goods once, whether it's in book publishing or newspapers or magazines, they'll feel far happier about asking you again, and they'll take more time to listen to your future suggestions.

If you can win a newspaper or magazine editor's trust to such a degree that he's ringing you once a week with a commission for an article, you'll have laid a very solid foundation stone for your future career. Imagine how much time and effort would have to go into approaching enough new people with enough ideas to get one a week commissioned. It would probably take a whole week, plus the day needed to write the article. This way it only takes the day needed for the actual work because all the marketing groundwork has been done in the past.

You need to make your name as familiar to potential customers as possible. There are a number of ways of achieving this and they'll all cost you time and money. Let's look at these methods of marketing yourself.

## Direct Mail

*Telecoms*
*Japan*

Write a letter that can be adapted to a wide range of different editors. It should be as short and to the point as possible. Explain you're a freelance writer and what your specialities are. Ask them if they have any work you could help them out with. Try to think of an angle that will differentiate you from the crowd. Are you willing to travel anywhere in pursuit of a story, for instance?

Tell them what you've had published, listing the magazines that have taken your work and asking if they would be interested in seeing any of it before commissioning you.

If you have a piece that you're particularly proud of, include it in the package.

You could send it either by post or e-mail. E-mail will be cheaper but once they've read it and clicked on to something else there's nothing to keep you in their minds. If you use the post they may file it for future reference, or leave it lying on their desks, where someone else might notice it and contact you.

With direct mail success comes down to sheer force of numbers. If you send out a hundred letters and only receive one commission as a result, it's still been worth doing.

Sometimes you'll get a delayed reaction. On occasion people have contacted me a year or more after they've received my initial approach, having genuinely put it in the files and then come across it later.

I've also sometimes invested in printed brochures listing all the publications I've worked for and all the different areas I'm experienced in. I've then mailed them to several hundred potential employers. It's hard work and quite expensive but has always paid dividends in the end.

## Advertising

Because it's expensive, advertising is a high-risk strategy. You could spend several hundred pounds placing an ad in a daily paper and by the following day it's lining guinea-pig cages. If you don't get an instant result your money has gone.

Over the years I've advertised in a number of different media and have concluded that it's only worth doing if you can afford to keep it up for a sustained period.

As a travel writer I advertised in publications like the *UK Press Gazette*, announcing what destinations I was planning to visit and asking if anyone needed any articles. In one case it led to the editor of a travel-trade magazine buying material from me every month for several years. It also resulted in a few tourist authorities and airlines offering me trips, which led to more articles. (For more on travel writing, see Chapter Twelve.)

For business and management writing I took ads in the advertising and public relations trade papers, which resulted in a reasonable flow of work, although not as much as from using direct mail. (For more on business writing, see Chapter Eleven.)

For my ghostwriting services I've been advertising in *The Bookseller* for around ten years. Sometimes the ad brings no response for months on end, but then one job will come in which will more than compensate for the money spent. I used the same advertisement in *Publishing News* for a while, as well as in *Publisher's Weekly*, the American equivalent. I advertised for a while in *Variety* to reach the denizens of Hollywood and again received a reasonable response. (For more on ghost-writing, see Chapter Sixteen.)

The ad in *The Bookseller* has meant that my name and telephone number are continually in front of publishers, editors, librarians, agents and booksellers. If anyone asks them if they know of a ghostwriter I'm the one they think of.

## Public Relations

If you can raise your profile by having articles written about you and your work it's always going to be helpful. It can also help in your local area if you can make personal appearances, whether it's giving talks at schools or women's institutes, or signing books in local bookshops.

If you have any success, like having a book published, make sure your local paper knows about it. They'll almost certainly be happy to publish a picture of you and the book and write a few words about your career and about the subject matter.

Apart from the fact that it might lead to a few sales of the book it'll also bring you to the attention of other potential employers in the area. (For more about promoting your books, see Chapter Twenty-Two.)

## Sales Promotion Stunts

When I was looking for business writing work I mocked up an exact copy of an article from *Campaign,* a highly reputable advertising business magazine. I replaced the picture of whoever the article was about with a picture of myself and the text with an article about me and the sort of work I did. I sent the article, with a covering letter, to every prospective customer I could think of. (If the recipients looked closely there was a small disclaimer in the bottom corner where the name of the publication should have been, saying 'not *Campaign'*.)

The style was very distinctive. All the recipients would have recognised it at a glance and would have made certain assumptions even if they didn't get round to reading all the glowing praise for my work in the body of the text.

The piece served a number of purposes. It caught the eye of my target market and put my name and face in front of them. It showed them I could write and it gave them details of my career. For those who studied it carefully there was the added benefit that it made them laugh when they realised it was a spoof. It resulted in a publisher giving me a two-book contract and a number of magazine editors commissioning pieces.

## Marketing Through a Website

Earlier I touched on the value of having a website on the Internet (see 'Do You Need Your Own Website?', p.33) and it certainly can play a part in your marketing mix. It's unlikely, however, that many people will stumble across it by accident, as there's too much material out there in cyberspace. But, if you can guide people to it, it will provide a sort of permanent brochure for your work. I have a site, which can be accessed through both http://www.andrewcrofts.com and http://www.ghostwriting.co.uk. So some people come across it when they go looking for a ghostwriter. More importantly, I can put the website address in my advertisements or give it to anyone who might ring me and ask for details of my work. They can then access it at their leisure, or without me even knowing they're doing so, and decide whether or not my services would suit their needs. I can update the site regularly to add anything that I think will be of interest to potential customers.

## Using Your Work to Get More Work

As soon as you've had something published you're immediately in a much stronger position for getting other work. Until that moment you're just one of the millions who want to be a writer, a tough place to be. Once your article has been published, make copies and include them in any mailing you're sending out to new editors. If you've had several published, just enclose a sample and tell them what other publications you've appeared in.

Always send out clean, new copies. Nothing looks worse than yellowing pages of dog-eared newspaper, giving way at the folds.

If you're applying for a specific job and they ask you to send some samples of your work, it can do no harm to send a large number. They probably won't read them all in detail but they'll immediately be able to see you have a track record.

Think of these samples as disposable, because editors don't have time to return them. Always keep the originals in reasonable condition so that you can make more copies when needed.

If you're able to scan them into a computer and e-mail them to potential clients that would be even better, although you must be careful not to send them in such an arbitrary manner that it becomes junk mail.

If you have a website, include any articles you have written (after checking with the publication involved that they don't object) for others to see.

## Giving Your Work Legs

Every project could lead to something else if you think about it laterally. If you've written a book on car maintenance you could use that fact to sell the idea of writing articles on the same subject. Send copies of the book to editors who might be interested and suggest a list of possible subjects. Make sure they understand you're looking to sell them these articles, not providing them as publicity for the book (although that is also a perfectly valid thing to do – see Chapter Twenty-Two).

If you've written a number of articles on a subject, you could use them to convince a publisher that you should expand them into a book. Send a selection of articles with your synopsis. They'll give you credibility as an expert on the subject and prove you can write.

Equally, you could send a book or articles to television and radio producers, suggesting you should convert them into a show or a series of shows.

Never think of any project as an end in itself – it must always be a stepping stone to something else.

## Reselling Your Material

There isn't a journalist in the world who hasn't 'topped and tailed' an old article and resold it to another publication. Provided you don't sell something to two editors who are competing in the same area, and provided you make at least some cosmetic changes, there's nothing wrong with repackaging good material and selling it to different sectors of the market.

Whenever you've had a successful sale, think of ways of repackaging the same idea and selling it to someone else. (In those circumstances it would be unwise to send editors a copy of the original article as they will always prefer to think they're the first in line.) You have invested heavily in time and effort to put together the material for any piece of work, always look for other ways to exploit it.

# CHAPTER SEVEN

# Finding Material

*'I write for women who read in the goddam subways on the way home from work. I know who they are, because that's who I used to be. They want to press their noses against the windows of other people's houses and get a look at the parties they'll never be invited to, the dresses they'll never get to wear, the lives they'll never live, the guys they'll never fuck.'*
Jacqueline Susann

In Chapter Three I looked at the potential subject material you already have at your fingertips. Now I will explain how to move on to the next stage: finding material that will keep you going once you have taken your first steps.

Whatever you're writing you're always going to need new ideas and material. Often doing the writing isn't as hard as finding a regular supply of stories that will interest editors or producers and the general public.

The whole world is your potential hunting ground and the further afield you're prepared to travel the bigger the game will be. But let's start locally.

## Stories You Already Know About

Think about all the people you've met recently. What was it about them that interested you? Did they have unusual jobs? Were they living in unusual houses? Had they suffered from a terrible illness or did they talk about some holiday from hell that made you laugh? Are they keen gardeners? Have they built an amazing tree house for their children? Do they breed dogs or budgerigars? Could they provide you with expert insights into any subject at all? Do you know of someone who's made a recent dramatic change of career, going from being a hairdresser to a firewoman, perhaps, or traffic warden to crop duster?

Do you know of a school that's doing particularly good work with difficult children and might be of interest to an educational supplement? What about a local touring theatre company? In exchange for the chance of some publicity they might allow you to join their troupe for a while or be backstage during some productions. You could then sell the resulting article to local papers in every town they went to after that.

## Finding Stories in the Media and Digging Deeper

Read everything with an eye to finding out more. If you see a small piece in a local paper about someone who's just returned from a round-the-world trip, contact them and ask if they'd like to do a more in-depth piece which you will try to sell to other magazines or newspapers. A small announcement in a daily paper about someone winning a prize for the size of their sunflowers might well become a full-length feature for a gardening magazine.

## Let People Know You're Looking for Material

If there's a local theatre or art gallery or museum in your area, let them know you're always on the lookout for new material. Many years ago I did that and a fringe theatre in London rang me up to say they had a young playwright acting in her own first play and suggested I interview her. She was very shy but, they assured me, she was very talented and had a big future. Her name was Victoria Wood.

Public relations people always want articles written about their clients. Make sure they know how to contact you, so that they can tip you off if something is happening which might lead to a story. For any number of stories that come to nothing, one may be a winner.

When an author brings out a book the public relations department at the publishers will want to get the writer interviewed as widely as possible. If they're a big name then there'll be no problem attracting the national papers and the chat shows. Even if they're not famous but have interesting things to say, they may provide a useful source of feature material for you.

## Don't Limit Yourself to One Country

We're lucky to have a language that a large part of the world speaks. Even if you limit yourself to one language, you still don't have to limit yourself to one country. The international community often comes to Britain when they're looking for good writers of English. In my ghostwriting career alone I've written autobiographies for an African chief, a Chinese billionaire living in Kuala Lumpur, a Bulgarian multimillionaire hiding out in the Swiss Alps, a Hollywood actress passing through the South of France and a technology guru living in a beach house in Bermuda.

There have also been the British residents who've gone off to have adventures in other countries, returning home with tales to make the toes curl. Over the past ten years I've written books with a Gurkha colonel who built an orphanage in Croatia, a Milton Keynes housewife who rescued children in Romania after the fall of the communists, a Birmingham schoolgirl who was sold as a child bride by her father in the Yemen, a nurse who worked in a orphanage for baby gorillas in the Congo and a grandmother, married to an Iraqi, who was in Baghdad when the Allied forces attacked. International spies, drug dealers, courtesans, gangsters, socialites, Egyptologists and heiresses have all called at some stage in search of a writer to help them out, and many of these enquiries have resulted in publishing contracts.

## Hunting on the Net

The Internet provides another source of stories as well as facilities for research; virtually everything you could ever want to find out is out there somewhere. The difficulty is sorting the wood from the trees. The majority of information available is erroneous at best, and always needs to be double-checked unless it comes from a known source.

To set off on the Net for a few hours of exploration, however, is a great deal less time- and money-consuming than heading out to the Congo or down the Nile. For writers who want to practise their craft in the privacy of their own homes and to venture out into the dangerous outside world as infrequently as possible, the Net offers a whole new universe of possibilities and opportunities. For most of our profession, though, it should only be a tool, not our entire world. If we don't get out and taste the real world ourselves occasionally we'll soon run out of inspiration.

## Using Written Material

It's always a great relief to find that someone has already written a book or article on precisely the subject you have to cover, so that you can read up on it. But where do you draw the line between learning from the text and copying it?

You can use the best bits as quotes; for example, 'as Professor Humpkin says in his book on the Peruvian Indians . . .' But bear in mind that if you quote from a published work at any length, its publisher may require payment. For the most part, however, you should study the book or article and then supplement it with as many other sources as possible. Just as a university student will study a textbook and then write a thesis on the subject it covers, you can study your sources, perhaps making bullet-point notes which do not plagiarise the actual words of the original, and then communicate the contents to your readers.

Once you feel you've understood the subject, you can write about it in your own words, pursuing your own slant, and perhaps mixing and matching the theories and findings of two or more experts.

As a writer, you are selling *your* understanding of a subject and *your* ability to communicate it. If you slavishly copy someone else's work, you'll not only be putting yourself in the wrong legally, but you'll also be doing a very poor job, because it will mean you haven't fully got to grips with the subject.

## How Much Research is Enough?

One of the differences between amateurs and professionals is that professionals have to know when something is 'good enough'. If you keep on polishing until a piece of work is perfect – which it never is – you'll never be able to make a living.

'Don't believe everything you read in the papers' is a cliché, but a true one. It's not that journalists and writers deliberately set out to mislead anyone – well not usually, anyway. It's just that they're often expressing their subjective opinions, or those of the people they've interviewed. Pressure of time means their research is never as extensive as it should be, and sometimes they'll be misled by interested parties. Something you read in a paper is as likely to be inaccurate or one-sided as something you hear in a classroom, at a dinner party or on a bus.

At some stage a writer has to decide that they know enough about a subject to write usefully on it. The more quickly they can reach that stage the more cost-effective it will be. If you're being paid £200 for an article, you can't spend weeks researching it – it's as simple as that.

This doesn't mean you can get away without thorough research, because anything that's under-researched won't sell. It just means you need to use the most efficient methods of gathering information. At the beginning of your career you'll have to do more research on everything you write about because you're still relatively inexperienced and so it will be harder to persuade editors to use you.

But when you've researched a subject once, you can write additional articles later, when new information becomes available. There are always demanding readers looking for the latest information.

## Adapting One Idea a Dozen Different Ways

There are a limited number of great ideas in the world, but an unlimited number of ways in which to angle them.

Imagine you've come across a local factory, Bloggs and Co, which manufactures plastic ballpoint pens with pictures of nude women on them and sells them to the Bangkok tourist industry.

To the local paper you write: 'Bloggs and Co are one of the big success stories in the area, creating local employment and bringing money into the country by exporting the girlie equivalent of coals to Newcastle.'

To business management and marketing magazines you offer a different story, about 'Bloggs and Co, who've taken the idea of marketing to its extremes and made it work. They researched a market need and set out to fulfil it, beating all the international competition in the process.'

To a left-wing broadsheet newspaper you could present a piece on 'a wealthy Western company cynically exploiting human weaknesses and cheating local Third World pen manufacturers out of business that should rightfully be theirs'.

For a national tabloid newspaper the suggestion might be along the lines of 'British birds are still the best, it's official! Even the Bangkok sex industry looks to Britain for its pin-ups!'

The example is flippant, but the principle is sound. There is always more than one way to look at every story.

## Doing Interviews

Interviewing is a useful skill. Most of the material you need to be a writer is in other people's heads. These people also provide the colour and the character that makes any piece of writing come alive.

### Who to interview

There are people you'll interview because you can sell anything about them many times over. They're the big names, the pop stars and movie stars. Just to get something from them assures you of a sale.

Then there are the less obvious people with something new or interesting to say. I once targeted a series of government ministers. They were not senior members of the Cabinet, or the ones with the highest profiles, so they were quite happy to give some time to a journalist. I was able to turn the resulting articles into a series in a general business magazine, and resold them as individual articles to trade papers for industries that those ministers had an impact upon. By finding a number of different outlets I was able to make as much from the interviews as I would have got by interviewing someone more famous for just one outlet.

In addition there are the people you interview because they have information you need to understand a subject. If you're writing a piece about modern philosophy you'll need to interview some modern philosophers to give the piece credibility and to learn about the subject.

Unless you're writing in your own area of expertise, you're always going to be finding out about a subject just ahead of your readers; a bit like a teacher swatting up on tomorrow's lessons to stay ahead of the class.

## Telephone interviews

Sometimes you'll only have a few questions to ask, and won't need any background colour, in which case you can do the interview over the phone. A telephone conversation will never be as effective as a face-to-face one, but it isn't always cost-effective to spend half a day or a day travelling to meet someone from whom you're only going to get a few paragraphs.

If you're about to do a telephone interview and the interviewee asks how long it's likely to take, say, 'Just a few minutes.' If they prove to have nothing to say you can then escape quickly. If they prove to have a great deal to say they'll soon get into their stride and forget the time.

If they seem to be fruitful sources of information, but they don't have time to speak to you when you ring, ask when it would be convenient to ring back – and make sure you do. This can have a number of advantages:

- It flatters them by showing you genuinely value their opinion.

- It gives them time to think about the subject and to come up with more thoughtful answers.

- It gives you time to talk to other people and increase your own knowledge of the subject.

For a full-length article on a subject you might need to talk to half a dozen experts. You might have a list of names and numbers, all of which you ring in succession, only to find that none of them are available. You leave lots of messages, and then nothing happens. So you panic and ring six more people, achieving only a modicum of success and begin to despair of ever getting enough material for your article.

Be patient, because suddenly you'll find they're all calling you back at the end of the day, or the following morning, and you're being given enough material to write a book. Talk to all of them, even when you think you have enough material, and try to include as many of them as possible in the finished piece. Try putting put what one said to the others: 'So-and-so told me such-and-such. Would you agree?' That way you can check you aren't going to print anything that is too wide of the mark. You may also be able to stir up some controversy, which always makes for good copy.

## Prepare your questions in advance

Always know what you want to find out in advance. There's nothing worse than sitting down with the interviewee and realising you haven't got a clue what to ask them. If you've been commissioned by an editor, ask for any background material they already have. If they don't have any, then find some yourself from a reference work or on the Net. Once the conversation is up and running you'll find it easy to think what to ask next. But if you can't think of anything then it's probably time to end the interview.

## Be familiar with your cassette recorder

Make sure you know how to operate your recorder with confidence. Always put in fresh batteries and have more than enough cassettes. You don't want to make your subject self-conscious by fumbling around with an unfamiliar machine while they wait to begin speaking.

Have a pad and pen as well because while they're talking you may suddenly think of something you want to ask them and need to jot it down. Otherwise, not wanting to interrupt their flow, you'll remain silent and perhaps forget what you wanted to ask.

## What to ask

In many cases the questions you want to ask are the ones the interviewee wants to answer. If you're writing about a new hotel the manager is going to want to tell you all about it. No problem there.

Sometimes, however, there are areas that you have to cover because an editor has told you to, but you know the subject will clam up. Always leave the difficult questions to the last and preface them with some disclaimer, explaining that you find it as distasteful as they do, 'but people are bound to want to know the truth', or something like that.

Have a list of prepared questions just in case you dry up, but don't hesitate to deviate away from it if the interviewee starts saying anything interesting.

If you're feeling nervous about the meeting, prepare a lot of questions in advance, in case your mind becomes clouded by stage fright and you need a prompt to refer to. Most face-to-face interviews last about an hour, so you need enough questions to fill that amount of time if you're hoping for an article of a decent length. If you dry up in the first five minutes the rest of the allotted time is going to drag by very slowly indeed.

Never ask closed questions, which can be answered with a simple 'yes' or 'no', otherwise you'll soon run out of steam and won't come away with any useful material. Closed question: 'Do you enjoy sport?' Open question: 'Which sports do you enjoy most?' Follow-up question: 'Why is that?'

## Always confess your ignorance

If your subject says something you don't understand, or use a term you're unfamiliar with, be quick to ask them what they mean. If you pretend to understand, in the hope of finding out later, you may have begun to lose the thread of what's being said. You'll also have given them a false impression of the extent of your knowledge. If you don't stop and ask for an explanation they may use more and more jargon, and start to talk on more complex levels, until you get completely lost.

As you gain more experience you'll become more knowledgeable about certain fields, and will at least learn enough about them to carry on sensible conversations with the real experts. Sometimes it can be a good idea to play a bit dumber than you are, just to get the interviewee to explain things in more depth in their own words. The clearer they can make their arguments the clearer your eventual article is going to be – and clarity is one of the most important goals to aim at, whoever you're writing for.

### Don't be afraid to ask rude questions

Many of us are reluctant to ask people direct questions, especially about really interesting things like money, sex, age or scandalous behaviour. One of the perks of being a writer, however, is a licence to be nosy. You can ask people how much money they make, what their private lives are like or anything else you're interested in. If they become upset you can apologise and blame your profession.

Most people, when asked a straight question, will not only give a straight answer but will usually do so with good humour. If they refuse to answer it's often simply because they haven't got anything interesting to say.

### Where to meet

If possible, meet your subject in their own home or office. They'll be more relaxed and you'll see them in their natural surroundings. If they don't want to do that, then hotel lobbies are useful venues, anonymous but usually quiet enough to record in, and quite relaxing. You can just order coffee or move on to a meal if things are going well.

Sometimes it helps to suggest an unusual meeting place, somewhere where they'll be forced to interact with other people perhaps, or one that takes them out of their usual comfort zone. It'll give you more to write about, although there's the danger of throwing them off balance if they don't feel secure.

## Putting your subject at ease

The chances are that whoever you're meeting will be nervous too. They have a lot more to gain or lose by this encounter than you. You're going to be making judgements about them in the media, quoting them and controlling the impression they make on the reader. That will make them uncomfortable.

Do everything you can to put them at their ease. Don't launch straight into questioning them like a television inter-rogator. Start with at least some small talk about your journey to get there, the surroundings or even the weather. It doesn't have to be anything scintillatingly witty, but if you can relax your subject they'll very quickly show you the way in which they want the conversation to go. And that is what it should be, a conversation.

If you're sitting next to someone at a dinner party and you allow them to talk about themselves and their views all evening, they'll go away with the impression you're an immensely charming and intelligent conversationalist. Very few people prefer listening to talking, and that's where you'll be able to gain your advantage.

You need to stimulate the interviewee, through questions and suggestions that they accept or reject, into giving you an insight into their field.

A good way to start the conversation might be to tell them what you think the theme of the article is going to be, and then ask them if they agree that is the best approach. Whether they think it is or not, you can follow up with further questions and then at least both of you feel you're working to the same agenda.

## Going 'off the record'

Once they've started talking, most people will relax and forget you're intending to write an article. They may then start to talk 'off the record'. If they tell you that is the case, then you should respect their request, otherwise you'll never be able to go back to them for more information. Only if they trust you not to embarrass them will they tell you the really juicy bits of scandal.

Either you can use what they say without attributing it to

them, or you can ask someone else, who isn't afraid to be quoted, if they agree with whatever it is they've said, and then quote this second person.

If they feel sufficiently comfortable, the interviewee will start answering your questions as if they have met you at a dinner party. Suddenly, as you near the end of the conversation – probably when you ask them how to spell something or to give you their full title – the awful truth will dawn on them that their words may be quoted in the press. They begin to wonder if what they've said might upset their bosses, friends or customers and they panic.

## Avoid showing them the copy

This is when they sometimes ask to see the copy before it's published, so they can 'check the facts'. While it might make sense to do this if you're hoping to build any sort of future relationship with the interviewee, it's not always practical.

Nobody can resist changing something, even if it's only a little something, when they see it in black and white. But if you've talked to six or seven people for a 1000-word article, you won't have time to send copies to all of them and then incorporate their corrections, even using e-mail.

There will be cases, however, where you genuinely need to check you're on the right lines, or where you have a vested interest in building a relationship of mutual trust, or where the person is just too important and powerful for you to refuse.

If you don't want to get into an argument with them, but don't want to let them see the copy either, try replying, 'I'm not sure what the editor's policy is on that, but I'll ask.' If later they repeat the request for a sight of the piece, just say, 'I'll tell the editor you want to see a copy', and leave it at that.

## Never argue

Unless the point of the interview is to be antagonistic it's never a good idea to argue with an interviewee or try to convince them of the error of their ways. You're there to find out about them and their views, not to convert them to yours. If you give them a hard time they may well clam up and then you won't have a story. If they see you as a sympathetic listener they'll relax and open up. They must never feel you're judging them, but they must be convinced you're fascinated by their every utterance. The more convinced they are of that, the more revealing they are likely to become.

## Coaxing the interviewee to perform

What you want to get from your subject is a performance. You want them to be informative and entertaining. You want them to tell you secrets that will thrill your editor and your readers. You want them to lift the curtain and allow you to peek into their private world. To do that you must allow them centre stage and not try to compete. You can always add your own voice and personality when you come to write the piece later. At the interview stage you want to get as much life and colour from the interviewee as you can.

## Never fear silence

Don't be afraid of leaving silences. Firstly because it gives the impression you're thinking about what your subject has said, and secondly because they may well feel the need to cover the silence by blurting out something more interesting than they intended.

## The nightmare of the time limit

The worst thing is to be given a draconian time limit. Sometimes it's unavoidable. If a Hollywood star is promoting a film they'll be ensconced in a hotel room and interviewers will be wheeled in and out by minders at ten- or fifteen-minute intervals. It gives you no chance whatsoever to relax and find any common ground; you only have time to talk to them about the product they're promoting (which is one of the reasons it's been arranged as it has). If the star is big enough your editor will still want you to do it, if only because they don't want to be the only paper in town who doesn't have something on the story. In these situations you've become part of the publicity machine and there's little you can do to improve the situation, apart from trying to think of some original line of questioning, which is almost impossible with someone giving dozens of interviews a day.

Interviewees of lesser status will also tell you they can only spare 'half an hour' or 'a few minutes'. Don't argue with them, just thank them politely and rest assured that once you've got them talking on their favourite topic they'll be happy to keep going for as long as you want to listen.

## Building contacts

If you're planning to write frequently about a particular topic, then it pays to build relationships with people who are good sources of information on it. Send them copies of the article once it's published with a note thanking them for their help.

Contacts through interviews can also lead to public relations and corporate work (see Chapter Eleven). So it's worth getting into casual conversation, explaining that you're freelance and that you do a lot of writing in their particular field. If they show the slightest interest, offer to send them details. If you have nothing printed, just write them a letter so that they'll have your name and number and website address to hand should they ever need the services of a writer.

Always keep people's names, titles, telephone numbers and addresses on file. By building a network of contacts, you start to cut down on the time and effort required for future jobs.

If you know which areas you're going to specialise in, it's worth starting files of press cuttings, keeping anything relevant that appears in the various media, including material from the Internet (which you can keep on the computer or print out). That way you'll have names of potential interviewees when you need them. You'll have to be selective, otherwise you could end up spending more time filing than writing. In some cases, however, simply compiling information may provide an income, since you can then create reference works, or lists of contacts to go at the end of articles that offer practical advice.

You might also be able to see new angles on stories by looking through the cuttings and recognising trends and developments. You might find, for instance, that one of the sources you've quoted in the past is now saying the exact opposite. You could then find out why their views have changed and build that into a new story.

## Using quotes

It's always safer to put statements into quotation marks if you're not entirely sure you agree with them. If you state them as facts, you lay yourself open to being proved wrong. If, on the other hand, you say, 'Many people in the industry believe such and such' and go on to quote someone to illustrate the point, then you have transferred any culpability to them.

For instance, unless you have a thorough knowledge of the industry, you're probably not qualified to assert that the 'widget industry is in decline and unlikely to recover'. It would be better to use an attributed quote: '"The widget industry is in decline," says John Smith, Chairman of Widgets International, "and unlikely to recover."'

To get this sort of quote you simply need to have asked John Smith a question such as 'What state is the widget industry in?' Once you have Mr Smith's opinion you can then go to one of his competitors and say, 'John Smith says ...' His rival may then agree or disagree, which gives you another quote and, depending on the answer, builds either a case or a controversy.

# CHAPTER EIGHT

# Writing for Newspapers

*'Throw yourself into the hurly-burly of life. It doesn't matter how many mistakes you make, what unhappiness you have to undergo. It is all your material ... Don't wait for experience to come to you; go out after experience. Experience is your material.'*

W. Somerset Maugham

Newspapers are a highly competitive medium, but they are also a lucrative market, since they publish so much material every day of the week.

## Local Papers

Although it's good to aim high, at the beginning of your career you shouldn't ignore your local newspaper. Local stories are easier to find and the local media are hungrier for whatever you can give them.

If you ring a local editor and ask if they need any freelance help, they'll probably say they have all the staff and material they need. It's still worth making the call, just in case you reach them at exactly the moment they realise they need an extra pair of hands. The fact that they aren't looking for freelance material at present doesn't mean they wouldn't buy something if it were good enough. The only golden rule is that the story must have local interest. It must quote local people.

## Following National Stories

Take a look at what's being reported in the national media. Is there a nationwide farming slump? Then get round to a few local farmers and ask if it's affecting them and, if so, how. Have crime figures risen again nationally? What about in your area? Do the local police have any statistics? (They probably won't give you quotes, but you never know.) Does the local council have any information? What about people in the street? Are publicans having more trouble with drunks? Are they hiring more door staff and bouncers? Ask enough people the same questions and you'll see a story forming in front of your eyes.

## Finding Local Characters

Local news is all about people. If you can find people who are doing unusual things or have interesting memories you have a story, particularly if you can link it to a specific event. Is there someone in an old people's home who's about to celebrate their hundredth birthday? Get invited to the party and interview them about what they remember from their childhood – even better if they've always lived in the area and can remember a time before cars, hamburgers and antibiotics.

Look in the small ads of the local paper and find people offering unusual services: rat catchers, palm readers, feng shui consultants, ladies of the night.

## The National Papers

Many writers aspire to writing for the national press, believing it will give them credibility. They're right – although the amount of credibility they gain will depend on the newspaper concerned and the material they supply to it.

Appearing regularly in one of the country's major dailies is an excellent springboard for anything else you might want to do. It can help you get television work, book contracts and other journalism and business writing work.

A lot of pages are produced each day by these papers, which have to be covered in words created by somebody. They constantly need new and interesting ideas for editorial. The difficulty is that they have a great many staff writers and reporters who need to be kept permanently occupied. They also have access to established, or even famous, experts on almost any topic they're likely to cover. However, if they really like or need your ideas or stories, they'll pay generously for them.

## What Do They Want?

Most national papers will be willing to pay for a story that's so original they haven't thought it up for themselves. But it's no good suggesting an interview with the Prime Minister or the US President unless you have some exceptional personal access or have got them to confess something totally new, because editors have staff who can do this for them already.

If, however, you've just returned from a one-man expedition to the South Pole, or have completed some research into why people get married which has revealed some startling facts about love, lust and the human condition, or have been held hostage in the Afghan desert for five years, then you have an advantage over anyone who works for the newspaper full-time.

Editors also like powerful, opinionated pieces that fit in with the prejudices of their readers. You can then become their resident misogynist or misanthrope, right-wing or left-wing loony.

## Selling Specialist Knowledge

Try offering editors specialist knowledge of one particular subject. Ideally, you will then be adopted as the paper's technology correspondent, gardening correspondent, astrology correspondent or whatever sort of specialist is needed. Once you've achieved that you have become an expert, and can start selling your wares to the rest of the media on the strength of it.

Once you're known to an editor as a source of material on a particular subject, and trusted to produce copy on time, they'll frequently ring you with urgent jobs. They nearly always need the copy delivered within a few hours because they want to use it while the topic is still hot. You need to be able to respond quickly to a phone call and be e-mailing them copy almost immediately. Usually there won't be time for much research beyond a few cursory phone calls to your existing contacts.

## How to Approach Newspapers

Keep submitting ideas for articles you would like to write as well as articles you've already written. Don't send anything that doesn't fit into the newspaper's readership profile. Editors on both national and local papers are very short of time and do not tolerate fools gladly. If you inundate them with unsuitable material they'll soon tell you to go away.

Do not send anything that you know, in your heart, is inferior, in the hope that they'll edit it into shape. They certainly will edit it, but only if they can see at a glance that it's useful to them.

When you're sending ideas, keep them short; no more than one paragraph laying out the idea and why it would interest their readers. For example: 'The average person sneezes or blows their nose 100,000 times in their lifetime. Would you be interested in an article on the effects that this has on the brain, based on new medical evidence, since it is a subject that affects every one of us?'

## Investigative Stories

If you've managed to uncover something which would either be impossible for another reporter to follow up in time (your aunt has been the Pope's mistress for fifty years and is finally ready to tell all), or would be extremely expensive for editors to put their own people on to (you've been working in the filing department of MI5 for twenty years and have compiled a list of all known terrorists working in Britain), then you have a commodity for which you should be able to demand a premium price.

Some freelancers do nothing but investigative reporting – usually writers who've spent some years working on national papers full-time and therefore know how to dig out a story that others would prefer to keep hidden.

If the story appeals to editors in America and mainland Europe as well as Britain, it may earn you enough money to live on for some time. When Andrew Morton found himself being fed information by Princess Diana for the book which would effectively change the British people's perception of their royal family for ever, he must have known that he'd found a story that could set him up financially. At the same time he also had to face the possibility that the world wouldn't believe what he was telling them and that the establishment would succeed in silencing him as they had silenced every other writer up until then. To get any good investigative story is bound to take a long time and there is always the danger that it will turn out to be time wasted. There is also no telling how long it will be before another story that good comes your way.

This is a hard line of business to be in. It requires a great deal of luck, and a lot of time spent in the right circles listening to gossip and rumour and then searching for the facts to back up your suspicions.

Occasionally you may come across juicy stories while pursuing some other project, such as a biography. You then have a double incentive to get into the nationals, since any coverage of the story will help you sell your book, as well as earning you the fee from the newspaper.

## Syndication

Because America has fewer national newspapers than Britain, syndication is big business there. Local papers are spread across the country to serve the needs of separate readerships and there is little or no overlap of readership, so papers in all the different cities and states can publish the same material – if it's relevant – at the same time. Some of the best-known columnists can end up making a great deal of money because they can sell one article to as many as 200 different outlets. However, the article has to be as relevant to readers in New Orleans as it is to readers in New York or San Francisco.

The same principles can apply in other countries, but on a far smaller scale. In Britain, which is so well served by its national press, there are only a handful of local daily papers. Some of these, like London's *Evening Standard*, are very powerful publications. The rest of the local press consists of weekly titles, which have virtually no budget with which to pay freelancers and very little interest in anything that comes from outside their geographic areas.

None of the editors will mind you selling your articles to other papers, as long as there's no overlap of readership. It's wise, however, when you win a new customer, to let all your existing outlets know about it, in case there's some conflict of interest that you know nothing about. For instance, several papers in different areas may be owned by the same company.

Initially, you should contact every editor separately and sell them the idea or article. No contracts or even letters of acceptance will normally be exchanged unless you're entering into a regular relationship whereby you agree to supply something every week or month.

If an editor asks you to sign a contract which would give them sole rights to the article and would stop you selling it to anyone else, decline to sign it. However, this situation is very unlikely to occur. As long as you ensure the article does not appear in directly competing media everyone will be happy.

To make syndication worthwhile, you need to be able to supply regular columns, not one-off articles. The amount of time and money you would have to invest in sending or e-mailing individual articles to local editors would not justify the occasional small fees you would be paid. If, however, you can persuade an editor to take a column every week, say, you then have a regular flow of income and a ready-made product, which you can offer to other, non-competing publications.

The sort of non-local subjects that are most useful to local newspaper editors are practical advice pieces. If you can produce a gardening column that tells people what they should be doing every week of the year, or a DIY column that covers a different topic in each edition, or an advice column on personal finance, then your words will be relevant to readers wherever they live.

## Doing the Deal

At the beginning of your career you will probably have to accept whatever rates the newspapers is offering, as you will not be in a position to haggle. As soon as they commission an article from you, or agree to buy something you have sent in on spec, ask them how much they will be paying. Make a note of that amount and ask them to confirm it in writing. Even if they don't get round to doing that, you should confirm it to them in an e-mail or letter, so that at least something is recorded. They are buying dozens of articles every day and, if you don't confirm them, details like agreed prices may well have been forgotten by the time payment is due.

## Take Photographs Whenever Possible

Pictures will always help to sell a local story. You don't have to be a photographic genius to take a shot good enough to illustrate your story, particularly if it's a portrait of someone you've interviewed.

## The Frustrations

Even when you've succeeded in selling an article to a newspaper editor, there may still be problems to deal with. Let's take a look at the ones you're most likely to experience.

### They decide not to use your article

Editors often agree to buy articles and then don't use them, because they don't have the space or something bigger and better comes along. If they've commissioned the work from you then they're still obliged to pay a fee, although it may be reduced if they haven't used the piece. You will then be free to offer it to rival papers. If you've sent it in on spec and they say they will use it, but then don't, they'll have a moral obligation to pay you for it since you haven't been able to sell it elsewhere while they were planning to run it. Whether or not the paper will honour that obligation will depend on your relationship with the editor. Provided you deal with them firmly and politely, they'll probably part with the fee.

### They edit your article down to nothing

Often editors get their staff to cut down an article so that it fits into an allotted space. Unless you've agreed the price at the beginning, you may then get paid a much smaller 'per word' fee. If you do agree a price when they first accept the piece, it's best to have something in writing, even if it is only an e-mail from you to the editor confirming the deal.

Unlike local newspapers, the nationals have plenty of money, and in most cases they would rather honour their obligations, provided they think you're being fair to them. Aim to build such friendly relations with the editor that misunderstandings are kept to a minimum and can be sorted out in a few minutes over the phone.

### They change your meaning

Editors are capable of editing your words so heavily that an article ends up saying something completely different from what you intended. If they're printing things under your name that you disagree with, it may annoy you a great deal. In such cases it's sometimes worth writing a letter to the editor to register your displeasure – preferably without endangering the relationship for the future. On the other hand, newspapers are such ephemeral things that you would probably be wiser to forget it, because everyone else will.

If they do change your article completely, you should then be able to sell the original to someone else, as it bears no relation to the piece that's been published. If you have a good relationship with the editor, you could tell them that you're doing this. Provided you're not selling to a direct rival, they're not likely to complain.

# CHAPTER NINE

# Writing for Magazines

*'The aim, if reached or not, makes great the life;*
*Try to be Shakespeare, leave the rest to fate.'*
Robert Browning

Magazines come in all shapes and sizes. There are more than 8000 of them on the market in Britain and they all need to get their material from someone. There is no reason why that someone shouldn't be you.

## National Magazines

Women's magazines and, increasingly, men's magazines, are a steady source of income for many writers. They don't need material in such vast quantities as the daily papers, particularly if they come out monthly, but they do require new and exciting material to compete with rivals. The money isn't as good as the papers pay, but you get to write at more length and the published piece will look smarter in your portfolio.

Always be on the lookout for new outlets for your work, whether it's in-flight magazines, give-aways on street corners, or piles of dog-eared back numbers in the waiting rooms of doctors' and dentists' surgeries.

## Special Features

All newspapers and magazines run special features to help them bring in advertisers. This means they dedicate a number of pages to a specific topic or place. In a national paper it might be anything from a Third World country to a city or the nuclear industry. A marketing magazine might run special features on conference organisation, corporate hospitality, marketing on the Internet, exhibitions or sales promotion. They then need to find a certain number of articles to justify calling it a special feature, and this makes them desperate for freelance help.

These special features usually come round at least once and sometimes twice a year. The staff writers very quickly run out of enthusiasm for writing about the same old subjects, so a freelancer who can think up new ideas on old topics, or provide interesting material to fit their ideas, is going to be very popular indeed.

Most publications produce lists of forthcoming special features at the beginning of each year. These are available from their advertising departments and are also collated by some enterprising firms and circulated regularly to interested parties. In some cases they can be found by visiting the publication's website.

If you have a great deal of material on a subject – say the motor industry – it would be worth finding out when magazines are doing special features on cars, and then sending them a list of suggested angles you could cover for them. You'll find many of them very grateful indeed.

## Local Magazines

Newspapers aren't the only local printed media. There are also the glossy county magazines, small parish and village magazines, newsletters put out by churches or estate agents or major local employers. Schools and universities have their own publications, which are mostly put together by pupils or students but might take outside contributions relevant to their readership. Anyone who has the job of producing printed material on a regular basis is a potential customer for a freelance writer. It may be that they won't be able to pay you, but at least you'll be getting published and you'll be building up a stock of stories and gaining experience.

## Celebrity Magazines

Celebrities are big business and there's a large market for pieces that are totally uncritical, which talk about whatever the celebrity wants to talk about – the clothes they wear to premieres, their beautiful homes, their love for their partners, children and mothers, the charity work they tirelessly perform for those less fortunate than themselves.

The market for this sort of material has grown massively with the burgeoning of celebrity titles such as *Hello!* and *OK*. If you can gain access to the stars and win their confidence, then they'll be happy to supply you with this material at times when they have records, films, books or charitable causes to promote.

If you develop a reputation with the editors as being someone who can bring the stars in, they'll be happy to pay handsomely for anything you manage to get, particularly if you can give them some sort of scoop or new angle. Some celebrities are better at supplying these than others.

You may also find that the celebrities themselves – particularly soap opera and sports stars who are eager to cash in on their fame before it fades – will be willing to work with you on exclusives once they know and trust you. They may agree to talk exclusively to you about their marriage break-ups or their exits from the closet on the understanding that you'll share the proceeds of the story with them. (This work comes close to ghostwriting, which I cover in detail in Chapter Sixteen.)

## Make Contact with Your Trade Media

Approach your trade media and suggest subjects for articles, or submit articles on spec. Every trade paper needs new and fresh ideas because the editors are limited in the number of subjects they can write about. If your specialist knowledge is to do with garden furniture and you can think of some good feature articles on the subject, the relevant trade publications will be desperate to hear from you.

## Clinching the Deal

As with newspapers, to begin with you'll have to take whatever the magazine's standard rates are. State in writing the price that you have verbally agreed with the editor, and, ideally, get them to confirm it in writing as well.

# CHAPTER TEN

# Writing Non-Fiction Books

*'Stop thinking of writing as Art. Think of it as work.'* Paddy Chayefsky

Non-fiction books are a tremendous potential market for free-lance writers because, unlike fiction, they can be tailored to any number of niche audiences, making it easier for publishers to see ways in which they will be able to market the final product. Even so, it's still a highly competitive field.

## Expert Books

If you have a great deal of information on any one subject, think about putting it into book form, particularly if you already have a reputation as an expert to back it up.

The market for 'expert books' is enormous, with some of them, like the cookery and gardening titles, topping the best-seller lists for weeks at a time. Any sort of self-help book, whether it is practical DIY or pop psychology, will find a market, as will books about the military or about good parenting. Everyone needs advice from experts at various stages of their lives.

Don't write the whole book yet. Just produce a document that will convince editors to commission you (see Chapter Five). But there's no harm in working on the manuscript whenever you have spare time, so that you are ready with something to show them when they ask.

## Prepare a Synopsis

Start thinking about ways of packaging your expertise in book form as soon as possible. Work up a synopsis that you can show to agents and publishers. Listen to anything they might have to say which will develop your idea or move you on to new ones. It may be that you can eventually produce a series of books on your subject, particularly if you become known to the general public through television. Popular cooks and gardeners can command six-figure publishing advances (these are discussed below) if they have good agents working for them.

You need to show potential publishers that your book is going to be different from the competition. Tell them what the unique selling points will be. For instance, is it aimed at total beginners or at more experienced readers? What are your strengths as the author? Are you the foremost expert in your field? What makes you the best person to write this book?

## Writing to Commission

There are times when publishers decide they want a book on a certain subject and then commission a writer to create it. Make sure that your name is known to all the publishers working in fields that you would be interested in. (For more on promoting yourself, see Chapter Six.)

## Biography and Autobiography

I will talk in more detail about ghostwriting in Chapter Sixteen. Suffice it to say here that most big celebrities would rather use a writer they already know and trust to help with their autobiography than bring in a stranger to do the job of being their spokesperson. But there is also the biography market. If you're always mixing in the celebrity world it's not hard to get hold of the background material needed to produce a biography.

If you've established a reputation as a show business journalist, publishers will be very happy to listen to any proposals you might have for biographies, either authorised or unauthorised, of famous names.

There's always a market for biographies of popular or controversial people, as well as of historical figures or the recently deceased. A biography of a controversial film star, athlete, pop singer, criminal or politician can be an enormous potential earner for both the publisher and the writer.

If you approach a commissioning editor with an idea for a biography, they'll want to know that you have a genuine enthusiasm for that person and that you have access to information that will give the book a particular selling point. This could be that you have unearthed something about the subject no one knew before, or that you have more information than any other writer, or that you have the subject's co-operation.

Biographies range from mighty works on people like George Bernard Shaw and Charles Dickens, which may take years of scholarly research to put together, to paperback biographies of twenty-year-old pop stars, which take a few weeks to research and then disappear from the shelves as quickly as the stars disappear from our television screens.

Which end of the market you work in will obviously depend on your personal tastes and abilities, and also on the material you have access to. If you're well known to a number of record companies, have a background in pop music journalism or know one of the celebrities personally, then you'll find it relatively easy to write 60,000 words, or whatever is required, that will appeal to fans. If you're a sports or political writer, known to the stars and to their friends and families, you'll be able to write about them with particular authority, and will know who to approach for help and background information.

## Authorised or Unauthorised

There are two schools of thought about whether an 'authorised' or an 'unauthorised' account is the purest form of biography. Publishers use either term as a positive selling point.

The authorised biography has the blessing of the subject.

This suggests they have given the author more information than would have been available to an unauthorised biographer. It also suggests the subject has had a say in what can and can't be included. The book may, therefore, seem censored to some readers.

The 'unauthorised' label on a biography suggests either that the subject did not think the writer was of sufficient importance to merit any of their time, or that there is something in the book which the subject would prefer to suppress. It can also mean that the book has been put together hastily from a collection of press cuttings to cash in on a sudden surge in the subject's popularity.

Often the only reason why stars withhold their co-operation from biographers is that they're hoping to write autobiographies themselves later and don't want their pitch queered.

The surest way to interest an editor in an idea for a biography is to be able to demonstrate you have a personal relationship with the subject, or at least their agreement to co-operate; access to at least one person close to the subject; and access to new and, ideally, controversial information.

## Approaching the Publisher for an Advance

The biggest financial hurdle for writers is raising money to live on while they write something they can sell. One of the best ways is to persuade a publisher to give you an advance payment, set against the royalties your book is expected to earn for you.

It's easier to persuade publishers to pay advances on non-fiction projects than fiction ones. They're less nervous about buying non-fiction because it's easier for them to influence the final shape of the book and they can predict more easily what audience it's likely to appeal to.

They also know that even if the author does a sub-standard job, they'll probably still be able to render it publishable by editing and rewriting, which would be much harder with a work of fiction.

## What is an Advance?

When you sign a contract with a publisher they promise to pay you a percentage of the money that the book earns – roughly ten per cent of the cover price. If they're confident they'll sell a certain amount they'll offer to 'advance' you some money on the strength of your synopsis and sample material.

Typically, they will pay you a third of that money when they sign the contract, a third when you deliver the manuscript and a third when they publish, although this will vary. As well as predicting the number of copies they think they can sell, they will also look at the possibilities of selling foreign rights, serial rights, film rights and so forth before coming up with a figure to offer you (see Chapter Twenty).

How much they offer will also depend on whether they're the only publisher interested in the project. In an ideal world – for the writer, that is – the agent will be able to get an auction going, with two or more publishers competing to win the book by offering larger and larger advances.

Once you've received an advance you have to repay it only if you fail to write the book. Even if it never sells a single copy, you get to keep the money. So publishers need to be pretty sure they can recoup their costs before they will be willing to shell out. You then don't earn any royalties until the advance has been recouped. Very often large advances are never 'earned out' through sales, but the writer will have been paid enough money to make the whole exercise worthwhile, the book is at least in print with the chance of becoming a runaway hit and the publishers are committed to pushing it because they want to earn their money back.

To persuade a publisher to pay you an advance, therefore, you have to convince them that:

- The book will sell well.

- You are the person to write it.

- If they don't pay an advance they may lose it.

- If they pay you up front you will deliver what you promise.

# CHAPTER ELEVEN

# Writing for the Business World

*'I am not a snob, but rich people are often a lot more fun to write about.'*
Noel Coward

The business community uses up a lot of words, and not always in the right order. It is in constant need of professional help and pays handsomely for it.

## Good Money and Interesting Stories

It may be that the money you earn from business writing will keep you in business while you establish yourself in other areas. Working for this sector may also give you an insight into worlds you would never have gained access to any other way. I've hung out with billionaires and millionaires and infamous entrepreneurs all over the world. I would never have enjoyed such unfettered access if I had not been writing for them. To infiltrate this world and discover its secrets, a little subterfuge is sometimes needed. If taking the shilling of the corporate world offends your creative sensibilities, try looking at it another way; see yourself as a spy, changing your appearance like a chameleon to understand the enemy better, so that one day you will be able to shed more light on their nefarious goings-on.

## Are You Selling Out?

Fay Weldon, the highly respected novelist, threw the critics into a fluster when she accepted a commission from the jewellers Bulgari to write a book that mentioned their name a certain number of times in a favourable light. She has made no secret of the pact and it seems an imaginative way of supplementing the publishing pot from the pockets of some of the world's fat cats. If the book is no good people will not buy it and so any contamination of the art of literature will be quickly stamped out. If it is good then that's reason enough to celebrate the deal.

We, however, are not yet at Ms Weldon's level and must start our search for corporate work further down the ladder.

## What Do They Need Written?

All business people need to communicate with one another, with their employees and with their customers. They need advertising, press releases, brochures, product information, company magazines, company histories, employee newspapers, corporate videos, training material, management speeches and reports, conference material, websites, direct-mail information, information on employee incentive schemes and on and on and on.

Most of them are not good at writing it themselves because they don't have time and they're too close to the subject. Also, they're used to talking in workplace shorthand, which means nothing to anyone else. Listen to a couple of management consultants discussing a client's problems and you'll see they have a language of their own. Any information they produce to persuade new clients to hire them, or to explain to existing clients what they should do to improve their businesses, will be unintelligible to anyone who's not steeped in the same culture as themselves. They need interpreters; people who can understand what they're saying and put it into a language comprehensible and interesting to others.

## Who Commissions the Work?

There aren't necessarily any specific job titles for the business people who hire outside writers. In a small or medium-sized company it's as likely to be the managing director or marketing director as a corporate affairs director or public relations manager. To narrow the market down you need to decide which market sectors are relevant to your experience and interests, and concentrate on these first.

An obvious starting point would be the many consultancies that offer communications as part of their package of services. There are public relations companies, corporate publishing companies, corporate communications advisers and general management consultants who include all these functions in their portfolio of skills.

Then there are the in-house public relations and communications departments within big companies, which would also include writing skills as part of their brief and might need the help of freelancers.

Start by visiting your library or local bookshop, or going online, and hunting out the best directory of public relations and management communications companies. You need names and addresses, either terrestrial or e-mail, and lots of them. To find one client you may have to approach a hundred companies.

## How to Approach Business Clients

I started by sending all the public relations consultancies a direct-mail letter and samples of articles I'd written for business magazines that I knew they would recognise. (Don't send too much material – you don't want to annoy them with thousands of articles; you can always offer them more later or guide them to your website, which can have as many pieces on it as you like.) I explained that my speciality was writing about complex subjects in laymen's terms.

It wasn't long before I had a roster of regular clients. The unexpected by-product of this was that I also gained access to many new ideas, which I could turn into articles to sell to business magazines. The more I appeared in reputable management publications, the higher my profile became in the corporate sector.

I then moved on to public relations officers in companies that seemed to be in the same subject area as the clients I'd worked on for the consultants. Then I added the big management and information technology consultancies. I offered to write articles they could place in the media, business books they could put their names to, corporate literature and employee communications. I was stunned by how much work there was to be had out there.

I found myself being sent all over the world to write about building projects for engineering companies, foreign markets for exporters and investment projects for financial consultants. I knew nothing about any of these subjects, but learnt all the time by asking questions and then earning my fees by explaining the answers to readers who knew even less than I did.

## What Can You Offer?

You're offering corporate clients your ability to ask the right questions, understand the answers and communicate those answers in the most effective way to their target audience.

You're selling your intelligence and your communication skills, and you package them up in the experience you've managed to cobble together along the way. If, for instance, you're an expert on office furniture and you've had a few articles published in trade magazines and other media, you can bring your knowledge to bear for manufacturers of office furniture, fixtures and fittings (of whom there are hundreds), and from there you can move on to other office equipment (pens, staplers, whatever you want), office layout designers and architects and to other branches of the furnishing industry. It's then a short hop to commercial property issues and on to residential property, home improvements, DIY and the rest.

When you make your living by writing, and enjoy doing so, it's easy to forget just how hard other people find the act of putting pen to paper (or words on screen). You are offering to take all that burden away from them, just as a commercial cleaning company is offering to keep the office loos sparkling and a recruitment agency will find them their staff, leaving them free to do whatever it is they're good at.

So, make them feel confident they're in safe hands.

## How Do You Charge for Your Work?

There are no golden rules here, so you have to work out your own scale of charges; one which is a realistic reflection of the rate you want for the job and also a rate clients will consider to be good value.

The business world works in a very different financial stratosphere from the magazine and book publishing industries. Companies are used to paying management consultants hundreds if not thousands of pounds a day without truly knowing what they're doing for their money. They're used to paying photographers similarly fantastic amounts to photograph their products and their factories. They're used to travelling business or first class wherever they go and claiming expenses for everything. Work out what your daily rate needs to be and then double it to allow for some haggling, though your clients probably won't haggle, since your daily rate will seem very modest to them. Alternatively, work out what you would get from a magazine for the same number of hours or words and double or treble that figure. Bear in mind that you're not overcharging them – it's just that magazine and book publishing pay appallingly badly by comparison.

# CHAPTER TWELVE

# Travel Writing

*'I can see now that my travels, as much as the act of writing, were ways of escape.'*
Graham Greene

Travel writing is a wonderful way to see the world, increase your experience, find new things to write about and, hopefully, make a bit of money. But how do you get the commissions to pay for the travel costs?

One of the great advantages of being freelance is having the freedom to travel wherever and whenever you choose. The only limitation is financial. But if you can earn money while you travel, and find other people who'll subsidise expenses such as flights, accommodation and car hire, even that difficulty is resolved.

What attracts many freelance travel writers is, first of all, the sheer pleasure of doing it, the excitement of visiting new places and enjoying new experiences. And then, the further you cast your net, the more likely you are to find interesting stories, and the wider your perspective will become. 'Travel broadens the mind' is a horrible cliché, but indisputably true.

## Be Willing to Take a Loss at the Beginning

The advantages are so great that it's well worth investing some time, and even some money, in getting yourself launched. You may recoup your costs very quickly, but it may also be that your first few trips don't pay for themselves. The worst that can happen is that you'll have had an interesting holiday. It's a risk you must be prepared to take because otherwise you'll have difficulty getting your first break. It may be you'll strike lucky and be offered an all-expenses-paid trip to Fiji from the first magazine you write to, but the odds are against it.

## Where Should You Go?

Decide on a destination and be determined to get there. It should be somewhere you already have an interest in and an ambition to visit. This project has to be a labour of love from the start.

If you write on religious topics go to a country that provides interesting material for books on theological thought and religious rituals. It could be the Vatican City or the voodoo worshippers of Haiti; it might be a religious carnival in Rio or a monastery in the Tibetan mountains. If cookery is your subject, you can go almost anywhere, although you're more likely to find unusual dishes to describe in South America or Burma than you are in France or Italy, where food writers have already trampled the ground for decades.

Choose somewhere as unusual as possible. In Tuscany or Benidorm you'll be visiting territory that's been written about a thousand times before.

Choose somewhere financially feasible. The first destination I chose was Hong Kong, at a time when flights to there were very competitively priced, so that I was confident I could afford to pay out of my own pocket if I had to.

Choose somewhere that has as many different angles as possible. At a beach resort there'll be a limited number of things you can write about. The capital city of a country that's not on the usual tourist map will provide a far wider variety of stories.

Your choice of destination may be guided by the sort of publications you already write for, or by the expertise you're known for. If your speciality is the building industry, for example, you could report on dam-building projects in Malaysia, skyscrapers in Hong Kong or hotel complexes in Honolulu. If you write about agricultural subjects, you could survey farming methods in a Third World country or food production on the Russian Steppes.

## Tell Everyone You're Going

Approach every single person on your media contact list, plus anyone else who'll listen, and tell them where you're planning to go. Ask what you can do for them while you're there. Suggest possible stories you could research or people you could interview. The more daring the suggestions the more likely you will be to catch their attention. Tell them you're going in search of the drug barons of Colombia and you'll elicit a better response than if you say you're going to tour the vineyards of France. A visit to the caves of Bin Laden in Afghanistan will score a great deal higher than a visit to the Eiffel Tower. You get the idea.

The advantage to editors is that they get a foreign story without having to pay the journalist's travel expenses, or at least only a part of them. If an editor from a building magazine needs a story about a new town being constructed in the Brazilian jungle, he has several options. He could try to find someone over there to visit the site, write it up and send the copy back. But where would he find such a person? How could he be sure of the quality of writing? How long would it take to arrive?

The next option is to go himself or send a staff writer. But the trip could take at least a week and might take more. He probably can't afford to be away that long on one story, and he almost certainly doesn't want to pay a staff writer a full week's expenses on top of their salary, just to have them away from the office for a week and then suffering from jet lag and an upset stomach for a week after that.

But suppose he knows of a freelance writer who'd be willing to tackle the story for the usual fee, plus a free flight and hotel. If he trusts the freelancer it looks like a good deal. The writer can afford to do the job because of the other articles he can sell to other outlets on returning.

## Think of Other Outlets for Your Work

As well as approaching all the obvious travel editors and travel trade press, think also about other media that would benefit from some travel pieces. For many years I wrote the travel column of a doctors' magazine. Every destination I went to I would write a piece for them. I would also write a piece on incentive travel (when a business sends its employees to exotic locations as a reward for reaching sales targets or some other goal) or conference travel for a marketing magazine and something for one of the travel trade magazines or in-flight journals. I regularly supplied articles about different export markets to an export magazine. Those core publications on their own would make the trip worth doing, so anything I managed to sell to national publications on top of that was pure profit. If *The Times* wanted a piece about opal fossicking in the Australian outback, I would include it in my itinerary. If I was offered a car rally across Israel I could offer the resulting pieces to a range of publications.

Do as much preparation as possible before you leave home. Write or e-mail the people you want to interview, explaining who you are and why you want to talk to them. Most people are very helpful to foreign writers, flattered that someone is travelling so far to see them and eager to be hospitable. If you leave it until you get there you may find they're unavailable, and you don't want to waste valuable travelling time on administrative tasks like setting up alternative interviews.

## Try to Get the Trip Subsidised

Once a few editors have expressed an interest in your trip you have something to sell to the authorities at the destination. Write to every airline that serves your route, telling them who you write for and what you plan to do, asking if they can provide you with a flight. (I used to offer to do business profiles of senior airline executives in management and business publications, which seemed to go down well.) Tour operators and holiday companies may also be willing to provide you with a passage to the destination on the understanding that you'll mention them in the final articles.

Write to the embassies and tourist authorities at your destination and ask if they can help you with accommodation, tour guides, information and general assistance. Just in case they can't help with the accommodation, write to the public relations departments of the hotel groups as well. It costs them very little to give you a room if the hotel isn't full and they'll like the idea of their venue being talked about in a conference or incentive travel magazine or holiday article.

If you're writing about business, contact organisations concerned with the promotion of business within the destination. They'll be keen to show you why people should be investing in their country, buying its goods and visiting it as tourists. If a country's main export is ground nuts, then the association of ground-nut producers will be pleased to help any writer who's going to profile their industry in a reputable publication.

All of these people like the idea of freelancers because they know the writer will only make money if he or she writes something. If they invite a staff writer from a national newspaper the journalist might produce something or might not, and may even write something detrimental. With freelancers they know they'll get more than one bite of the cherry and therefore stand a better chance of getting good coverage in exchange for their generosity and efforts.

Write to any British-based companies that you know to be active in the area you're going to, asking if they'd like any writing done. They might want something about their local branch for their head office magazine, or to send to a trade paper. Or they might just give you the name of someone out there who could help you with introductions.

On my first trip to Hong Kong I got a flight from an airline by writing a profile of the managing director, and a hotel agreed to put me up for a month at a very nominal rate. The tourist authority took care of transporting me around.

Encouraged, I went on to organise an island-hopping trip, lasting several weeks, in the Caribbean. Here the opportunities were even greater because every island had its own tourist authority (and some had their own little airlines as well).

## Educationals

Once the travel industry had established that I was a *bona fide* travel journalist I began to receive invitations for 'educational' trips. This is when a tourist authority or some other interested party invites a number of writers in a group to be taken around the destination and shown the tourist sights. The advantage of these assignments is that all the organisation is done for you, and you simply have to turn up at the airport with your passport and sun cream. The disadvantage is that you have less time and freedom to follow up the quirkier stories on your own, although the organisers will always do whatever they can to accommodate special requests.

With a combination of organised trips and independent travel, I managed to visit nearly every part of the world that interested me, particularly the Far East, the Caribbean and the South Pacific, areas that proved to be a mine of offbeat stories.

## Increase the Stop-Overs

Once a trip is finalised, see what other places you could visit at the same time. Organising a flight to New Zealand, for instance, I discovered the plane also stopped in Hawaii, Tahiti and Fiji. I contacted the relevant authorities in these islands, told them I was flying in and asked if they could make arrangements for me to stay a few days. They all agreed and I turned one destination into four with the investment of just a few more days of my time, making the trip far more profitable.

## Background Reading

The broader your background research the more intelligently you'll be able to write about the place, because you'll have a better idea of where to look for the angles and what questions to ask once you get there. This doesn't mean reading only dry history and geography books. Novels can be just as useful – and sometimes more so – in giving colour and life to a place both before you visit and while you're there.

The books don't have to be current, and they don't have to be particularly literary or learned. They just have to give you another insight into the place, stimulate your imagination and feed you ideas and perspectives that'll help you in your research.

I remember reading Graham Greene when I was in the Far East and Haiti, V.S. Naipaul in Trinidad, *The World of Susie Wong* when I was in Hong Kong, James Mitchener when I was in Hawaii and Herman Wouk's *Don't Stop the Carnival* in some tiny Caribbean backwater. A life of Gauguin gave me a different slant on Tahiti, and *The Thornbirds* on Australia. For almost every destination there's something by great travel writers like Jan Morris or Paul Theroux. Even a quite modest autobiography written by a local and read in a place like Penang or Jamaica or New Zealand would help me understand the cultures I was visiting so fleetingly. There's always plenty of time to read when you're travelling, sitting on planes or in airports, or hanging around hotels in the evenings. Don't waste a second of it.

## Look for Hidden Stories

Think laterally. There will always be stories for every kind of outlet if you think hard enough. A youth magazine will want to know about the clubbing scene in whatever city you go to, a brewing magazine might want to know about British-style pubs, a magazine for dog lovers might want to know about local breeds or an ecology publication might want a report on the local environment.

Every destination has its characters. In Haiti a hotel bar was still frequented by types who'd appeared in Graham Greene's *The Comedians*. In Hong Kong I found young British girls with careers they would never have been able to get into back home. In Jamaica Noel Coward's faithful retainers allowed us to look over the deceased author's house, which was just as he'd left it, his unfinished paintings still lying around his studio.

Interview anyone who's willing to talk, every scrap of information can add to your knowledge of the destination. Can you interview the country's president, or someone running a revolutionary party? Or a nun doing charity work in the slums? Or an English family running a hotel in the African bush? A women's magazine could be interested in a policewoman working in the Bangkok vice squad, a gay magazine might like a piece on a gay couple running a transvestite bar in Tahiti; a surfing magazine might like some background on people running beach businesses in Hawaii or Newquay, a golfing magazine is likely to want to know about golf courses everywhere, and will welcome comment from local professionals and managers.

However much you do on a trip, you'll only ever be able to scratch the surface of another culture in a short visit. But the more scratches you can make during your stay the more you're going to have to write about when you get home.

After a short trip to Israel, say, you might be able to break down the trip and offer a number of different pieces: 'Visiting Jerusalem/Tel Aviv/Bethlehem', 'Floating in the Dead Sea', 'Staying in a Kibbutz', 'Holidaying in a War Zone', 'Making the Desert Bloom'.

Then look at ways in which each of these subjects can be adapted to suit different outlets. A piece on the therapeutic powers of the Dead Sea might suit a health or medical magazine as well as the travel pages of a national paper. It could also be included in a general round-up of the whole tour in another magazine. A journal for the hotel industry might be interested to know how the hotels on the Dead Sea attract people to the lowest point on earth and create travel packages based on the health-giving properties of the water.

A piece on staying in a kibbutz could be of interest to a national paper or magazine as well as a publication aimed at students and young travellers. It might also be of interest to a farming or horticultural magazine, linking it to the 'Making the Desert Bloom' idea. If you spend some time thinking about the different permutations you'll be surprised by how many there are.

## Consider a Travel Book

Think also of the possibilities of compiling your discoveries in book form. A book on group travel opportunities for the business market perhaps, or the best beaches of the world, or a humorous look at island-hopping. They're all potential outlets for material and ways to make sure you're invited back.

## Stay Truthful

Because you've been given so much for nothing by your hosts, you may feel obliged to write favourably about everything you've seen and heard. They certainly hope you will, and they'll have shown you aspects of their countries that they hope you and your future readers will like. That does not mean, however, that you should be afraid to be truthful in what you write. Indeed, you'll find it impossible to sell sycophantic 'puff' pieces anyway.

Your duty is to write honestly and interestingly about everything you've experienced. If you've been commissioned to write a piece about the conference facilities on a South Sea island and they turn out to be non-existent, then you must say so. However, there's no reason why you shouldn't write another piece for a brides magazine about the suitability of the island as a honeymoon destination because of the intimacy of the hotels and the peaceful atmosphere.

There are always a number of facets to any destination, and just because you choose to write a piece about the scandal of child prostitution in Thailand for one magazine, this doesn't stop you writing another article praising the scenic beauties of the country or the wonders of the national cuisine.

Bear in mind that if you get a reputation solely as a muck-raking journalist you'll find it increasingly difficult to get people to help you finance trips. If, however, you succeed in finding and selling exposé stories, you should either be able to persuade editors to pay your expenses as you become more established, or raise your prices to cover the costs yourself.

## Making It Pay

Travel writing is very time-consuming. You have to be sure that the resulting writings are going to earn enough money to cover the time you spend 'on the road' as well as the time you spend at the screen after your return. To get the figures to balance, you need to squeeze every last ounce of material out of every trip.

Some writers are able to write while they're travelling, particularly now that we have laptops and e-mail. I personally find that hard. I'd rather concentrate on gathering material and then think about the writing once I'm back home. Travelling with a laptop also makes you vulnerable to theft. If you feel the same, then keep every bit of background material you can lay your hands on, along with cassettes, diaries, notebooks and whatever else you use to record your experiences, and sort it all out when you get home again.

# CHAPTER THIRTEEN

# Writing for the Spoken Word

*'Not every writer has it in him to write "the great American novel".
The trick is to do your best.'*
Sidney Sheldon

The spoken word is almost as big a potential market as the written one, and not only plays, films, television and radio dramas. People are talking all the time to audiences of all sizes, and to the media. Many of them need to have their words written for them by someone else.

## Who Needs Speechwriters?

Everyone from the President of the United States to a schoolgirl running for the position of head girl can benefit from professional help with their speeches. The difference between professionally written speeches and ordinary daily speech is most noticeable with politicians. When they stand in front of an autocue they become statesmanlike, eloquent and understandable. When they're caught off guard by the television cameras they're evasive, inconsistent and often incomprehensible.

The business world is equally full of people who have to make presentations, create an impact within a short space of time and get messages across to target audiences effectively. Some can write the speeches themselves, but most have neither the time nor the inclination and need to hire professionals.

Celebrities who sell their services as after-dinner speakers often need help to make themselves sound witty and worth the mighty fees they're charging. At any public function someone normally has to stand up and say something. A few are able to be spontaneously informative and entertaining, the rest have to work at it.

## Where to Start

Offer to help anyone you know, from the best man at a friend's wedding to children joining debating societies. Practise your skills and let people know it's what you do. You'll be surprised by how many will approach you for help and eventually you'll be able to charge for the service.

Once you know the sector of the market that suits you, you can target it with advertising and direct mail. *Private Eye*, for instance, carries ads from speechwriters, as do some of the magazines for senior management.

## Getting Their Voices Right

Writing a speech is akin to creating a monologue for a character in a drama. It's no good making them sound like you. If you're a twenty-five-year-old woman with a university degree in nuclear physics it's no good writing words that you'd want to use if they're going to be coming out of the mouth of a company chairman who left school at fourteen and made his money in scrap metal.

Imagine your clients as fictional characters and only use words they would use. Talk to them beforehand if possible to find out what they want to say and to listen to the way they speak. Don't give them phrases that will be hard to match to their accent.

## Making an Impact

Be very clear what a client's main messages are. If the audience goes away remembering only one thing from the speech, what should that be? If the media are going to pick one soundbite from it, what do they want that soundbite to say?

The problem with unscripted, everyday communication is that we're all thinking about too many different things at once. The message becomes muddled, in both what we say and what we hear. In scripted speeches we have an opportunity to clarify the messages that pass between us and make an impact.

Never be afraid to repeat key phrases, three times if necessary, and help the speaker to leave long pauses after making important points. Everyone talks too fast out of nervousness; anything you can do to slow down their delivery will help the audience to understand the piece.

## Writing for Your Own Voice

Try to think of ways to convert your writings into speeches you can deliver yourself. If you've just returned from living among tribesmen in New Guinea you'll almost certainly have a book in mind and a range of articles. A speech would be another way of using the material. It would also help to promote the book when the time comes.

Speaking your own words out loud will help you to improve your writing style. If words can't easily be spoken they're probably hard to read as well.

## Selling Your Talks

Once you have an interesting talk, approach as many societies, venues and clubs as you can find. You might want to limit yourself to a geographical area, or you might be willing to travel anywhere. Give them a brief outline of what you want to talk about, and enclose your book or articles if they've been published by that stage.

When you've spoken a few times you'll be surprised how word of mouth will spread and you'll receive invitations from organisations you didn't even know existed. There's nearly always someone in every audience who'll ask if you'll speak at another event. People who organise talks are keen members of other audiences, constantly scouting for new attractions. You can use the same talk over and over again because the majority of the audience will always be hearing it for the first time.

Once you have a script, contact radio and television producers to see if they'd be interested in having you to speak on their programmes, either doing your complete talk or being interviewed.

# CHAPTER FOURTEEN

# Writing Fiction

'Top Five Fastest Novelists
1. Jack Kerouac wrote The Subterraneans in three days. 2. George Simenon allowed himself six days to write a Maigret novel. 3. Walter Scott finished two Waverley novels in three weeks. 4. Ernest Hemingway, D.H. Lawrence and Evelyn Waugh each completed a novel in six weeks. 5. Anthony Burgess wrote five novels a year.'
Terence Blacker, from his novel about novel-writing, Kill Your Darlings

The unpublished (and probably unfinished) novel is as much a reality in the lives of professional freelance writers as it is for anyone else who lives, or would like to live, by their writing.

No marketing consultant will ever advise a client to create a product they like and then try to flog it to the world. It's generally considered to be commercial suicide. That said, many of our greatest products are the result of someone pursuing a dream with no interest in the realities of the marketplace. I doubt if anyone would have advised J.K. Rowling to commit quite so many words to paper on the off-chance that a publisher would be interested in her world of wizards and boarding schools.

Looking round any bookshop, you might think fiction is a far more popular form of writing than fact. It makes up about forty per cent of the book market and therefore should not be dismissed as a potential source of income for the freelancer.

The problem lies in the number of people who enter the fiction market, and in the fact that you'll almost always have to write the entire book on spec before anyone will make you a financial offer. Let's say it takes you six months to write (it could take six years, but for the sake of argument we'll pick a lower figure). Can you truly risk working for half a year without any money coming in at all? Probably not.

Whereas with non-fiction you can pick a specialist niche and persuade a publisher to back you during the writing process, with fiction you're competing with everyone in the world who thinks they have a book in them.

## The Allure of the Blockbuster

It's the dream of most writers to create a novel that sweeps to the top of the best-seller lists, perhaps even winning the Booker or Whitbread Prize along the way. These things do happen.

On the other hand, a Society of Authors survey showed that half its members earned an average of less than £5000 a year, considerably less in many cases. Although we read of £1-million advances, most novels take a year or more to write and earn a thousand or so pounds for the author. They vanish into the bookshops like water into the desert sand.

But every so often one of them inspires a publisher to pay a big advance to the author and finance a major marketing campaign, or a critic delivers such fulsome praise that people begin looking for the title, or word of mouth works its magic and a book rises from the swamp of fevered competition to become a best-seller. The odds, however, are very much against it, however beautifully you write.

## A Mixed-Risk Portfolio

Look at your career as an investment portfolio. You need some low-risk investments to provide quick, safe money; these would-be articles that have taken only a few days to write can be sold to a wide range of different titles and produce a few hundred pounds. Next come middle-risk investments, the projects that have been commissioned. The money may not be brilliant, but at least it's guaranteed and you know when it's coming in, so you can budget.

Then you need a few high-risk ventures because they're what make life worth living and give you something to dream about. If, however, you put all your money into a high-risk venture and it fails, it'll drag you down with it.

## Why are You Writing It?

It's good to have a project that you're deeply emotionally committed to, as long as you do not put so much time into it that you can't make a living.

- Be sure that you aren't just writing it for yourself. There must be something about the venture that will be of interest to other people.

- Will it take readers into places they know nothing about?

- Will it lift curtains on to hidden worlds?

- Will it make readers laugh?

- Will it make them desperate to know what happens next?

- Will they be able to sympathise with the characters and want to know more about them?

- Is there something about the story that will make them pick up your book rather than the several thousand others in the book-shop?

If the answer to all these questions is 'not really', then you're wasting your time. Writing the book might be good therapy for you, but it doesn't make good business sense. If you have to get it out of your system, fair enough, but the chances are you'll be even more hurt by rejection when the time comes to offer your baby to the marketplace, because it's been such a labour of love.

## Let's Improve the Odds a Little

It's possible that you're a literary genius. Unfortunately, literary genius is a quality in short supply, so the odds are always against any of us possessing it. You'd do better to concentrate on writing something commercially viable and letting the readers decide later whether it's a work of genius as well.

Once again, put yourself in the shoes of the publisher who's going to receive your manuscript. It's probably at least 100,000 words long, which means it's going to take up a great deal of time, firstly to read and then to show to other people in the company and to edit and print out if a decision is made to buy. If there is no marketing angle they'll be less inclined to make an offer. Is it possible to classify the work? Is it a thriller? Is it a crime novel? Is it a romantic saga? Is it horror or humour or sex?

Other categories come into vogue for a short while. There was the 'shopping and ****ing' genre, the 'Aga sagas' and the 'chick-lit' genre. It sounds cynical but it's reality. (I know, I know, your book would never fit into anything so vulgar as 'a category', and my name is Salman Rushdie too.)

By giving thought to the packaging and categorising of your fiction you're merely trying to find ways of attracting readers. People who like a particular genre will go to that section of the shop first. If your book has a chance of appealing to a wider audience, then word of mouth will attract other people to it. Publishers need to see who the potential readers are to make decisions about the sort of cover likely to catch their eye and the sort of marketing that will appeal to them.

Ask yourself next what it is about the book that readers will enjoy, so that you can tell the publisher in advance. Is it set in an exotic location? Is it funny, or exciting or sexy? Is it set in the world of Formula One racing or academia? Are the characters straight from the pages of *Fortune* or *Hello!*? Is it a modern Dickens or a modern Agatha Christie? Does it explore the mean streets of Manila or the fashionable salons of Paris? While you must avoid at all costs the use of clichés in your writing, you may well have to resort to them as shorthand in your marketing.

## Practise Writing Cover Blurbs

Look carefully at the blurb on the back of some of your favourite books. What was it that made you buy them? The setting? The characters? Now write a blurb for your book, and that will act as the initial synopsis you can send to publishers or agents, asking them if they'd like to see more. You could also write a longer synopsis, maybe two or three pages, which details the plot and characters – but not so much detail that someone skimming through it will get confused.

## The Opening Chapter

You must get the opening chapter right, and most importantly the opening page. If you can't grab the reader's attention on the first page, and probably in the first paragraph, the chances are they'll move on to something else.

Some writers become highly indignant when they discover a publisher only read the first few pages of their work before deciding to reject it. But they have no one but themselves to blame. If the first page isn't totally enthralling no one will read on. Why would they bother?

This is not just a question of creative writing technique; it's also a question of good marketing. The first taste of any book must be so delicious that the reader is unable to resist consuming the whole thing.

Get the blurb and the front page right and the chances are publishers will be willing to read the rest – they might even agree to offer a modest advance to help you as you write it.

When I had an idea for a comic novel with a serious theme called *Maisie's Amazing Maids*, based on the adventures of a ghostwriter, I prepared a synopsis which pointed out that, as an experienced ghostwriter myself, I would be able to provide an angle for the publisher to promote the book on. As a result the publisher was willing to pay an advance, just as he would have done for a non-fiction book. This is what I sent:

*Maisie's Amazing Maids*

### The Author
Andrew Crofts is one of Britain's most successful ghost-writers. Millions have read his books. Through his work he

mixes with spies and mercenaries, billionaires and slaves, rock stars and actors, courtesans and fraudsters, gangsters and gurus, eccentrics, saints and sinners of every kind.

In this fast-moving comic crime thriller he lifts the curtain on the hidden, colourful world of a leading ghostwriter with an international cast of clients.

### The Story

Joe Tye, an American ghostwriter currently living on the Bohemian side of London, receives a letter from a Filipino girl who claims someone has stolen her 'beautiful new breasts'.

His investigations uncover a string of girls in similar circumstances, all mysteriously answering to the name of 'Doris', and a cruel and callous trade in young bodies and lives. The horrors he discovers eventually threaten the one person he cares about more than any other – his eight-year-old son.

## Mixing Fact and Fiction

Another promotional angle is to 'fictionalise' true stories. The media can then talk about the book by writing about the true incident or the people in the story. It provides the writer with the opportunity to use their descriptive and story-telling powers, while also providing a basic framework on which to market the book.

This works best if the characters are famous, like Samuel Johnson perhaps, or infamous, like Jack the Ripper or Ned Kelly.

Using fictional devices like dialogue and description can help to bring historical stories to life, and they can also help to fill in factual gaps with speculation. With a researcher called Tom Freeman-Keel I wrote a book called *The Disappearing Duke*, which was based on the fifth Duke of Portland and a court battle over his family inheritance. Although there was a lot of historical evidence for the story, there was also a mystery surrounding the eccentric aristocrat, and the court case was full of lies and rumours. The fact that he was a real Victorian figure, and one of the richest men in the world, gave the synopsis an angle which appealed to publishers, while the fictional telling of the story made it less dry and more readable.

This is how the synopsis went:

*The Disappearing Duke* by Tom Freeman-Keel and Andrew Crofts

This is a true story in which the truth is tantalisingly elusive and the main character steeped in layers of deliberately manufactured mystery.

It's a work of historical detection, following a web of deception and intrigue that continued for over half a century and ended in a headline-grabbing court case. It centres around one of the greatest and most eccentric aristocratic families of the nineteenth century, the Cavendish-Bentincks, at a time when the British aristocracy were at their height of wealth and power.

It involves fratricide and disputed fortunes, secret underground passages and stately homes, mock burials and clandestine marriages, fraud and bribery, corruption and the financing of a prime minister, perjury and blackmail.

It is also the story of an establishment cover-up in which witnesses who were likely to expose the truth were cast into asylums or jailed.

*The Disappearing Duke* is partly a courtroom drama, starring some of the most distinguished aristocratic names of the Victorian era, and partly a mystery surrounding the life of the fifth Duke of Portland, one of the richest men of his time, and claims by his descendants that he led a double life. The Duke was one of the great eccentrics of Victorian England, building an underground palace beneath his stately home, Welbeck Abbey, which still exists today. There were rumours that he had killed his brother, who was in political cahoots with Benjamin Disraeli, and that he led a double life as Thomas Druce, the owner of a large department store in Baker Street. When his descendants started to fight for the title and immense fortune, they revealed layer upon layer of deception and scandal in the lives of both the Duke and Thomas Druce.

The book will appeal to the same readers who enjoyed the mix of history and mystery in *The Surgeon of Crowthorne* by Simon Winchester, *La Grande Thérèse* by Hilary Spurling and the many Jack the Ripper books. It will give insights into the bizarre and colourful lives of the rich and aristo-cratic in the same way as *Georgiana, Duchess of Devonshire* by Amanda Foreman, *Amphibious Thing – the Life of Lord Hervey* by Lucy Moore, *The Warwickshire Scandal* by Elizabeth Hamilton, *Aristocrats* by Stella Tillyard and the many other books which lift the curtain on glamorous and controversial historical figures of the last few centuries, from Oscar Wilde and Bosie Douglas to Fanny Burney and Mrs Jordan.

It will be written in a gripping, narrative style.

On another occasion I wrote a synopsis for an autobiography of a gangster called Norman Johnson who, in the 1970s, found himself having an affair with a Middle Eastern princess he was supposed to be guarding. We weren't able to find a publisher for the book as fact, but we got it commissioned as a fictional treatment of the same story. It came out as *The Princess and the Villain*.

## Selling Short Stories

It's even harder to sell short stories than it is to sell novels, since they only appear in book form once you've written enough for an anthology, and then you probably need to be famous to get the project off the ground. In most cases you need to adhere even more closely to the various genres, either writing for the women's magazine market or the equivalent men's titles. Study the magazines and then tailor your product to them. They know what they want and they always stick to their formulas. The chances of selling a literary short story, unless you already have a fan base, are next to negligible.

## Plant a Seed

Another way to justify the time taken writing a novel against the probable price that you will receive from the publisher is the possibility that it will lead on to other things. A novel is a seed that can, if it lands on fertile ground, grow into a magic tree that will give you everything you ever dreamed of. When Ian Fleming first wrote a spy thriller with a character named James Bond he can never have imagined just what a merchandising monster his creation would turn into. In Jeeves and Wooster, P.G. Wodehouse created characters who have been recreated by new actors so often and so successfully that they're familiar names to virtually every generation since Wodehouse wrote the originals.

A great fictional idea or character can live on for centuries (just look at all those Dickens, Austen and Trollope novels that continually turn up on television). Being an author of fiction is a bit like owning some Premium Bonds, never knowing when your number will come up and your book will be back in fashion.

## Other Fictional Avenues

Publishers sometimes commission 'novelisations' of successful films and television series. They give you the scripts and ask you to turn them into novels. They offer a fee, which will probably not be generous because they know the work will not take long, as you won't need any time to think up plots and characters.

Novelising can be a useful experience, and can provide an equally useful injection of funds during quiet periods.

There are also series of books, particularly in genres like horror, romance and erotica, where the publishers will commission writers to produce books to order. (Ghostwriting skills are relevant here – see Chapter Sixteen.) Your name will probably appear in small print on the book, but it will be sold on the brand awareness of the series. Publishers will generally approach people who already have a track record in the genre, but if you'd like to have a go for any particular series it could be worth contacting the editor in charge and sending them some sample chapters (or even a whole manuscript if you have the time). They may not buy that actual book but, if they like your style, they might ask you to write others to their specifications.

At the grander end of the market there are the 'sequels' to great novels such as *Gone with the Wind* and *Rebecca*, as well as commercial characters like James Bond, which publishers commission from well-known authors. If you have an idea for a sequel (or a 'prequel') to a favourite classic book then it might be worth approaching the publishers who own the rights and asking if they'd like to see an outline and some sample material.

# CHAPTER FIFTEEN

# Writing for Children

*'You must write for children in the same way as you do for adults,
only better.'*
                                                        Maxim Gorky

The moment the world realised J.K. Rowling had joined the
club of the wealthiest people in the world, everyone wanted to
follow in her footsteps. And anyone who has made up stories
for their children has thought about committing them to
paper. So why can't everyone do it? Well, because almost
anyone can make up a short story for children, the competition to move from amateur to professional is even greater than
in other areas of writing. To sit down and write a story for small
children which might have six words to the page looks a lot
easier than writing an adult novel. (I am now talking about
books for a younger age group than the Harry Potter stories.) So
millions of people give it a go and all their attempts pile up in
the offices of agents and publishers, most of them looking
virtually identical.

It's almost impossible to say why one children's character or
book should become a runaway success while another doesn't.
And that is why most of us can't do it. To be a success as a children's writer you must be able to think like a child. There
mustn't be the slightest trace of adult cynicism to be found in
the work. If you read any of the Harry Potter books, or
anything by Jacqueline Wilson, you'll find they're intelligent
novels written with as much attention to plot and character as
any of the adult equivalents. If you look at picture books for

younger children you will see that the most successful ones
have a simplicity that cannot be faked. Children know what
they like and no one can fool them into reading something
that isn't written from the heart.

## Create a Package

If you believe you could write for this market, then attack it
like you would any other sector. Create your characters.
Provide illustrations yourself or find an artist to work with.
Produce outlines for several books in the same series since children are faithful customers and will always buy more of the
same thing if they like it. Show the publishers that your idea
can be kept going, that it won't be a one-off.

## The Possible Merchandising Bonanza

Harry Potter isn't the first children's character to become big
merchandising business. When *Peter Pan* became a stage play
J.M. Barrie's book was transformed into an industry that would
continue to turn over money long after he'd died. A deal struck
with Disney over *Winnie the Pooh* at the turn of the millennium, more than seventy years after the books were written,
brought hundreds of millions of pounds into the coffers of the
owners of the rights. J.R.R. Tolkien's *Lord of the Rings* trilogy
returned to the front of the bookshops when the first of them
was filmed, nearly half a century after they were written. That
was a major remarketing and repackaging exercise, but more
modest television adaptations are happening all the time. The
rights to *Postman Pat* went for over £5 million to a merchandising company in 2001.

Although the stories are useful material, it is actually the
characters that become valuable. Modern scriptwriters can
create any number of new situations for Winnie the Pooh or
Paddington Bear, just as they can for James Bond or Sherlock
Holmes or Miss Marple. To create the product that will last for
ever you have to invent a memorable character, instantly
recognisable to everyone. Sometimes a children's book can

languish in obscurity for years before an animator or puppeteer picks it up. There has probably never been a character who's enjoyed such enormous and instant success as Harry Potter, and it may be a long while before another appears to rival him.

# CHAPTER SIXTEEN

# Ghostwriting

*'I'd like to have money. And I'd like to be a good writer. These two can come together, and I hope they will, but if that's too adorable, I'd rather have the money.'*
Dorothy Parker

There are several questions that regularly follow the conversational revelation that I'm a ghostwriter. 'Why on earth do you want to do that?' is usually the first puzzled response. 'Don't you resent someone else getting all the glory?' is the next, and then, 'So what famous people have you done?'

## A Ready Supply of Material

As we have already established, the fundamental problem facing any professional writer is finding a steady supply of ideas and subjects so dazzlingly certain to appeal to the book-buying public that publishers are bound to offer huge advances. One answer is to collaborate with other people who lack writing skills and experience but have great ideas and stories.

They might be celebrities who will impress publishers with their notoriety, or ordinary people who have undergone extraordinary experiences. Alternatively, they might be experts in subjects that the public want to know more about.

## The Money

A management guru I was interviewing for a business magazine suggested the deal to me. He'd been asked by a publisher to write a series of management books. The books would be good public relations for him, but he didn't have time to write them. He suggested that I should write them for him, having attended a few of his seminars and rifled through his filing cabinet.

'I'll get the glory,' he explained, 'and you'll get the money.'

In the screenwriting industry everything has to do with teamwork and collaboration. Why should the same principles not apply to book writing?

By using someone else's knowledge you can cut your research time for a book from a few months to a few days because you're going straight to the source of the material.

By ghosting books for other people, and hiding behind their names, a writer can produce far more books than the market could bear if they were appearing under his or her own name. It's quite possible to write a book of 100,000 words in two months if the material is immediately available to you, but you could never achieve such a fast turnaround if you had to do the research from scratch.

By having most of that output coming out under other people's names, the credibility problem is removed. No one will know quite how prolific you are and a few good ghosting projects each year could increase your earning potential considerably.

Most people in a position to require a ghostwriter can almost certainly command larger fees for their words than the people who do the ghosting for them. They'll probably be able to sell more books as well. As a result there will be more money in the pot and the ghost's share is always likely to be more than he or she could earn by writing the book on their own.

## What Glory?

As to not getting the 'glory' of being the sole author, any non-celebrity who's published a book knows how fleeting the glory is. Only the smallest percentage of books gets reviewed. Most vanish completely from the shelves within a few months of publication and are usually pretty hard to find even while they're on the market. Apart from those of a handful of literary stars (many of whom choose to write under pseudonyms anyway), few people recognise the names of authors. But when I wrote an autobiography of the *EastEnders* star Gillian Taylforth, who at the time was dominating every tabloid front page that Princess Diana wasn't, the book was written about in virtually every newspaper in the country and talked about on virtually every chat show that the publisher's publicity team could persuade the poor woman to go on. While Gillian was spending a week being shunted around all day from breakfast television to late-night television, I could stay comfortably at home and get on with my next project, content in the knowledge that the promotional side of the project was in the hands of a true mistress of the media. Nothing I could have said to any of those journalists or chat show hosts would ever have made the story such an attractive prospect as Gillian's media appearances did.

Sometimes the ghost's name will get mentioned on the cover of a book and sometimes it'll appear only on the flyleaf. Sometimes you'll get a mention in the acknowledgements and sometimes you won't appear at all. You may get billed as 'co-author', but it is more likely to say 'By Big Shot with Joe Bloggs' or 'as told to Joe Bloggs'. While it's never worth making a fuss about a credit, it is worth asking for a mention (or getting your agent to have it written into the contract), because other publishers may notice it and sometimes other people with stories to tell will write to you care of the publishers to see if you would be interested in working with them.

## The People You Get to Meet

Of all the advantages that ghosting offers, the greatest must be the opportunities to meet people of interest. Ghosting is a licence to ask the sort of questions that you truly want to know the answers to, and to be allowed inside some of the most extraordinary stories. It's about being able to step right inside other people's lives and then walk away at the end unscathed.

Ghosting is like being paid to be educated by the best teachers in the world. Imagine, for instance, being asked to ghost *The Origin of Species* for Darwin, or *The History of the Decline and Fall of the Roman Empire* for Gibbon. Imagine being paid to learn everything that's in the heads of these people and then turning their thoughts, words and notes into book form. Could there be a better form of education?

Of course, not all people who use ghostwriters are going to create books of such lasting value. But suppose your specialist area is information technology. If you get invited to ghost for one of the most famous innovators in the business you'll be able to ask questions about the future and learn things at their knee which other people would have to pay good money for in the form of consultancy or seminar fees.

## How to Do It

Many people would like a ghostwriter to write their life stories for them, or give flesh to the novels they've been thinking about but never got round to writing. Some of them might be prepared to pay for that service but almost none of them have a story a publisher would be interested in buying.

You need to attract the people who have the saleable stories without being inundated by those who don't. You could pick out individuals you're interested in and approach them directly. The chances of success are slight since you have to catch them at the moment when they're thinking of doing a book. There's also the problem that most celebrities already know a great many journalists that they'd be happy to work with. There's a strong chance you'll merely alert them to the idea of a ghosted autobiography and they'll then ring up a chum and suggest they do it, rather than go with someone they don't know.

Another approach is to make it known within the book trade that you're able and willing to undertake ghosting work. That way, whenever someone comes to a publisher or an agent with an idea for a book but an inability to write it, your name will pop into their mind as a possible collaborator.

Write to everyone you can think of in the industry, offering your services (see 'Direct Mail', p.63). Advertise if you can afford it (see 'Advertising', p.63). Get yourself a website (see 'Do You Need Your Own Website?', p.33).

## A Case History

Zana Muhsen, whose father had sold her as a child bride in the Yemen, went to her local library to find out about ghostwriters. The librarian obligingly looked me up in *The Bookseller*. After hearing Zana's story I wrote a synopsis and sample chapter of *Sold* and found an agent to represent it. The book was eventually translated into every possible language and it has so far sold over three million copies and spawned a sequel, *A Promise to Nadia*. In 1992 it was France's best-selling non-fiction title.

To get her story on tape Zana and I spent three days together in a hotel suite in Birmingham and I then spent two months writing. As with all the authors I ghost for, she had complete control over the text. Nothing was shown even to the agent until Zana had okayed it, but she changed almost nothing.

## Sharing an Agent

Having one good agent representing both parties in the arrangement, whose prime interest is in getting the book well published, not in encouraging the ghost and the author to fight one another for larger shares of the pot, means that I have almost never exchanged a cross word with any of my subjects. (For more on choosing an agent, see Chapter Nineteen.)

## Suppressed Ego

Ghostwriting is a matter of suppressing your own ego completely; a good discipline for any writer who isn't producing opinion pieces. You're fulfilling a similar function to a barrister in court, pleading the client's case. You listen to their story and then tell it for them, helping to get across their view of the world.

It's important to be interested in the person you're ghosting.

If they have nothing to say that you want to hear, the project will become an unbearable burden. Imagine spending that much time talking to someone who bores you, and then having to go away and write it out all over again.

It helps if the books are interesting at a number of different levels. Not only did writing *Sold* give me an insight into the alien culture of a peasant girl in the Yemen, but there was also the adventure element of whether Zana and her sister would escape, as well as the insights she gave into the way the diplomatic world allowed them to become victims of political expediency. It was one of the first books to talk about life behind the veil from the point of view of someone who'd experienced it, and it was all told in the voice of a straight-talking Birmingham girl. It was like a true version of an Arabian Nights tale and a nightmare that any young woman can understand.

As a well-known soap actress, Gillian Taylforth was in an altogether different world. She was a woman the tabloids couldn't leave alone, which gave her another dimension. On top of that she'd had the courage to take on News International in court. Even more amazingly, she'd lost and faced personal financial ruin, as well as ridicule everywhere she went. Despite all this she remained a resolutely charming and funny woman with a strong family around her. It had the makings of a Greek tragedy and worked at so many different levels that it was easy to find enough material.

## Catching the Voice

All the rules which govern shorter interviews (see 'Doing Interviews', p.74) apply even more to ghostwriting. It's essential for the ghost to make the subject feel completely comfortable. If they think the ghost is going to criticise them, judge them or argue with them, they won't relax, open up or talk honestly. It's not the ghost's job to change their opinions, but rather to encourage them to tell their story in the most interesting and coherent way possible. The ghost must be able to coax them off their hobby horse and persuade them to answer all the questions that readers are likely to ask.

Once the voice is on tape the ghost creates what amounts to an 80,000-word monologue, just as a playwright might do, staying completely in the author's character at all times, using the sort of vocabulary the author would use and expressing the same views, ideas and prejudices.

When Colonel Mark Cook asked me to ghost his book *A Promise of Hope*, about the rebuilding of an orphanage in Croatia and the effects the experience had on his family life, he was worried, having read *Sold*, that he'd come out sounding like Zana. I assured him that my goal was to make him sound like a public school-educated Gurkha colonel enjoying a mid-life crisis, not a fourteen-year-old Birmingham girl who's been white-slaved for eight years in the bandit-ridden mountains of North Yemen.

## Seeing the Structure

A ghost must also be able to see the structure of a book from early on in the process, and be able to package the concept so that an agent can sell it. He or she then needs to guide the subject into providing the right material, keeping them on track and clearing up any inconsistencies in the telling of the tale.

## How Do You Get Paid?

How you get paid will depend on how speculative the project is when you first become involved. If there's no publisher on board and you're going to have to produce a synopsis and sample chapter on spec, then it would be reasonable to charge a fee for that service, agreeing to make a new arrangement if the book became a reality.

If a publisher makes an offer, you could either agree a fee, which the subject will pay you, or you could suggest splitting the proceeds fifty-fifty. This way you'll both have wasted your time and energy equally if the book doesn't sell well, and will both be equally rewarded if it becomes a best-seller.

If the other party is a celebrity and it's obvious the book will make a large amount of money from serial rights or foreign sales, you might have to accept a lower percentage, or a percentage that will become lower once the subject has received a pre-agreed amount. For example, the proceeds might be split fifty-fifty until the ghost has received £50,000, at which stage his or her share might then drop to forty per cent, and might drop again at £100,000.

Often the money a publisher offers is not enough to make a difference to a celebrity. For many celebrities, having a book published offers more of a public relations benefit than a financial one. A film star's autobiography will help to sell the film they're in at the moment, and will remind Hollywood that the star is alive, well and bankable. For a business person, a book can enhance their credibility and that of their company. If someone in this position is approached by a ghost who's willing to do all the work, they'll probably be less interested in the money than in the speed and ease with which the book can be written. They may even have already had a go at writing it themselves and know how hard it is. If the ghost can convince them it will only take up a few days of their time to talk through the ideas and stories for the book, they may agree to whatever deal the ghost's agent suggests (although their lawyers may then put up a fight on their behalf, which is why it's always better to share an agent if possible).

If the project already has a publisher and the ghost is being asked to do no speculative work, then it may be that a fee will be suggested. In that case your agent will have to negotiate as high a fee as possible, with a small royalty on top perhaps. This way you'll have definite money, which will be a fair rate for the job, but you'll have lost the possibility of making huge money if the book is a runaway success.

The ideal situation is to have half your projects on a percentage basis and half on fees, because this gives you some guaranteed income as well as the excitement of the possible big win.

## What If It's a Vanity Publishing Project?

If someone wants their story told but is unlikely to get an offer from a publisher, you have to decide whether it's a story that's worth writing and how much you will need to charge them for the job. It's important to be honest with them about their chances of finding a publisher, and if they're still keen, then name your price. I've done several books in this way for very wealthy individuals who were able to purchase several thousand copies of the book for business purposes, or because they had a market for the book in another country, which made it a viable prospect for publishers.

But producing a family history or a personal memoir does not have to be the prerogative of the very rich. In these days of desktop publishing it's quite possible to produce on a computer at a reasonable price a book that will be of interest to a limited number of people. You could perhaps help these people, for a reasonable fee, to compile the information they have in their memories, their photo albums and their scrapbooks. It may be that they don't have enough for a full-length book, but you could help them turn the material into a presentable booklet of, say, 20,000 words.

## Reaching the Family History Market

To find customers interested in recording their family history you'll probably need to advertise your services in media read by older people, as they are the ones with the stronger inclination to record their lives. Some will just want you to collate material they've produced for themselves, while others will want the whole writing process taken off their hands. You will have to judge, and price, each project on its own merits and offer whatever services they feel they need.

## Ghosting Articles

Articles can also be ghosted. Business people will write articles to promote themselves, their companies and their products, using ghostwriters (see Chapter Eleven). There are also the celebrity columns in newspapers and magazines purporting to be by sports stars or socialites. These are normally written by staff writers on the papers, but if you make contact with a celebrity before they go to the paper you could arrange for them to put their name to material which can then be written by you and submitted on a freelance basis.

## Linking Articles with Books

There can also be a link between articles and books, since someone who has enough information for a number of articles may also be persuaded to put their name to a book, and someone who has authored a book will usually be interested in promoting it with articles. A ghost who's already familiar with the subject after writing a book will be a natural choice for writing the articles, and vice versa.

If you're receiving royalties for the book it will be in your interest to market and promote it in any way possible, and getting articles into the media (see 'Lighting the Fire' and 'Local Radio', pp.186–7) is one of the most effective methods of selling books. It may also be possible to write some of the articles used to promote the book under your own name, giving a more objective view of the author and the content. These intricate relationships are only possible, however, if there is a strong bond of mutual trust between the author, the ghost, the publisher and any magazine or newspaper editors involved.

If it's obvious that your role as a ghost will prejudice your journalistic judgement about the subject, then you should explain your situation to editors at the beginning. It may make one or two of them discount you as a reliable source, but others will see if as confirmation that you know your subject in depth.

## Be Totally Professional

One of the reasons why publishers like to use ghostwriters is that they know they'll be reliable. You must do nothing to damage this impression. They don't want to hear about any of the problems you might be having getting the story out of the subject; they just want to know that the book will arrive on time in a publishable form, conforming as nearly as possible to the synopsis or the brief.

Often the authors of the books are busy people and hard to

get hold of. Sometimes they're temperamental. The publishers consequently rely on ghosts to act as go-betweens to make the process as smooth as possible. By demonstrating skill, tact and diplomacy, the ghost increases the chances of securing further work from the publishers.

You are also the subject's best friend in the business. During the long months when the agent is trying to sell the project and the phone doesn't ring, you have to assure them that this is perfectly normal and doesn't mean that they will never find a publisher. When they're first presented with the manuscript and panic at seeing all their indiscretions laid out in black and white, you have to be the one to reassure them they can remove anything they want to before you show it to anyone else. (Once given the power to make changes they nearly always leave it virtually untouched. However, controversial issues can lead to a failure of nerve in the subject, and in this case the ghost may need to let the publisher or agent do the negotiating with them.)

When the publisher wants to change the title or favours a cover in the subject's least favourite colour, you will again have to be there to offer reassurance. When the book comes out and the subject can't find it on the front table in their local book-shop, you'll have to explain the economics of the business to them and try to dissuade them from ringing the publisher and ranting and raving. No one said it was going to be easy.

## Ghosting for Series

There is another form of ghosting in which the writer works to a brief to produce fictional books for a series, which is published under a fictitious name, or possibly the name of the author of the first book in the series.

Children's books, for example, often appear in series, some-times with as many as a hundred titles (see Chapter Fifteen). The books are written to very tight briefs, either with the same running characters or set in similar locations or situations. It might be a series set in a vet's practice, or stories about young girls and their ponies or boys and their favourite football clubs. The writers are not allowed to tamper too much, if at all, with a winning formula, however creative their ideas might be. These types of readers are very loyal once they find a format they enjoy and publishers like to be able to give them as many titles as they're willing to buy.

They can be enjoyable projects, a bit like school exercises. Although the financial rewards are usually low, if you're a relatively fast worker and can get the tone of the books right first time, they provide a fair daily rate of pay. If you're a new writer, projects of this kind provide excellent practice and allow you to build a relationship with a publisher, showing them that you're reliable and professional.

# CHAPTER SEVENTEEN

# Writing for Film, Television and Radio

*'One of the most common misperceptions of Hollywood is that it is rife with stories of overnight success. Nothing happens overnight, especially in this business. Every success, no matter how seemingly effortless, was coaxed and cajoled and, finally, extracted with tongs.'*
Hollywood television writer Rob Long, in his book
*Conversations with My Agent*

Working as a movie writer sounds glamorous, and just occasionally it is. In most cases the stars won't even know who you are, the producer will hire eight other writers to change everything you've produced and you'll only have one big hit project about every ten years, if you're lucky.

But if you have set your heart on it nothing will put you off, and there are a great many markets for scripts along the way before you get to the blockbusting movie.

## Getting Started

As with any sort of writing, the only way to start is to actually do it. People who buy scripts can only do so if they have something to look at.

Start by researching who the potential customers are and where to find them. The relevant areas are live theatre, radio, television and film. Any writer who doesn't intend to act as the producer for his or her own work is going to have to find a collaborator within the chosen medium. That collaborator, or champion, could be a producer, a studio executive, a director, an agent, or even a well-known actor in search of a vehicle. Whatever happens, someone else has to help get the idea to the stage where money is on the table to turn it into a film, play or programme. Your first step, therefore, is to win that ally. Most of these people are extremely busy and have dozens of approaches made to them every week.

You have to prepare something that will catch their attention; a piece of writing that distils your idea down to its essence and makes it irresistible.

If you can't get someone to buy your idea, you won't be able to get them to buy the final script either, so it's important to do a treatment or synopsis first. By making the treatment as attractive as possible you're also preparing the ground for the final product. The more work you do at this preliminary stage, whether you're creating a television game show, a documentary or a Hollywood blockbuster, the better the final product is likely to be and the better your chances of selling it.

Just like book publishers, the people you're selling the concept to need to see immediately how they will sell it to other people. They have to be able to persuade their colleagues to share their enthusiasm, financiers to back it and the public to watch it.

They must also persuade busy stars and directors to become involved in the project. It's no good being deep and esoteric at this stage. There are too many good ideas around for anyone to waste time trying to work out what you're trying to get at.

## Live Theatre

There are reference books listing theatre and production companies, but they'll only give you the bare bones of the information you need. Because a theatre company is listed doesn't mean they buy or perform material by modern writers, or that they would like the sort of thing you do. You need to find out what they are doing. Go to see their productions, ring them up and ask them what they want. Take a look at their website.

As well as the big theatre producers working on Broadway or in the West End of London, there are small touring theatre groups, local amateur dramatic clubs, theatres above pubs and in village halls, and university and school theatre groups. Any of these might be open to trying out a new play. If the treatment catches their attention, you can sit down and write the play itself – probably on spec.

Before any company looks at a play they need to know they can afford it. A touring theatre group with half a dozen actors and a Transit van is not going to be able to stage *The Lion King* or *Phantom of the Opera* in the same way as a West End theatre with a budget of millions.

Ideally, you should get to know the company and the actors before you write the piece, because you're much more likely to create something they like if you know what their taste is and how far their capabilities can stretch. If you're already living among them – at university, say – you have an advantage.

If you have no such network or connections, then you're going to be sending your material in cold to producers, just like a novelist submitting material to a publisher. The difference is that 125,000 new books a year are published and probably only a few dozen new plays. There are, however, fewer people in the race, which makes the odds slightly less terrible.

Even if the producers don't accept the play that you send in, if they can see something in your writing they like, they may well encourage you to try something else.

There is no easy way into this sector of the scriptwriting market. In fact the easiest way might be to produce the things yourself.

## Radio

Radio is a far less competitive medium, partly because it doesn't hold the glamour of its visual rivals. It's a great testing ground for ideas that might later be moved on to television, particularly comedy and quiz projects. Radio programmes are relatively cheap to make and so producers can sometimes be more experimental than their television counterparts.

Listen to the medium, find out who's producing the slots

you think your work would fit into, and then contact them. If they like your style they'll start to commission work from you.

## Television

Television is crammed with writers producing everything from concepts for new shows to the seemingly ad-libbed comments of quiz masters and announcers. There are one-off films and plays and also an enormous number of soap operas for all age groups at all times of the day and night. There are dramatic adaptations of famous books, documentary scripts, sitcoms and news programmes.

These all need a lot of writers, but they need them to be able to fit into moulds. There is room for exciting new ideas, just as in the other media, but that is probably not the way you'll break in.

Find out who's making the programmes you want to be part of, and then write something that will show them what you can do. There's no reason why you shouldn't try several different styles at the same time. You could do some sample scripts for *EastEnders*, *Emmerdale* and *Coronation Street* and send them to the producers. If they like what they see they'll ask you in to work alongside the established writers and you'll gradually find yourself becoming part of the team. You could write your own pilot for a sitcom and submit it to the comedy producers. They might buy it and commission a series from you, or, more likely, they'll invite you to talk through other possible ideas for series that you might like to think about.

You could create material with a specific comedian in mind and submit it to them via their agent at the same time as showing it to television stations. Or you might start by simply writing a few gags for a particular comic to perform on stage and make contact that way. A lot of comedians start out writing their own material, but sooner or later, if they're successful, they'll need the support of writers, particularly if they appear on television, a medium famed for eating up vast amounts of material.

If you have ideas for game shows, develop them and start submitting them, both to the big broadcasters and to the independent programme makers. Because it's an industry filled with similar ideas and concepts, there's a danger they may accidentally steal your ideas, so keep a copy and a note of when you wrote it, just in case.

Documentary makers need a steady supply of scriptwriters and they're always looking for people who can work fast. It's a very specialised skill, finding the right number of words to tell the story and fit into the few seconds that a particular image is on the screen. They also like to work to tough deadlines, sometimes sending out tapes in the morning and asking to have the completed scripts back by the evening.

## Film

Everyone wants to be in the movies – watch *The Player* by Robert Altman, or *Barton Fink* by the Coen brothers. But there is so much money at stake in financing a film that almost no one is going to take chances on anything that doesn't seem to be a sure-fire hit. There are a few brave mavericks out there making films that are different, but only a few, and everyone wants to get to them.

The best bets might be to create a property in the form of a book first (like J.K. Rowling or John Grisham) or to have a big star on your side, or to have access to tens of millions of dollars.

If you have none of these, then the next best thing you can do is keep sending your scripts to production companies. Again it's like buying lottery tickets, but every so often you'll manage to sell an option – which means a producer will pay you not to sell the idea to anyone else for a period of time, while they see if they can get the project going – or you'll find a producer or director who so loves your work they become your champion. It's always an outside chance, and you'll need to have other, more reliable sources of income at the same time, but that's no reason not to do it.

If you have a film in your head get it down on paper. But also get it down as a ten-page treatment and as a one-paragraph 'high concept' which you can put into a letter or an e-mail and hope will catch the producer's attention for a few fleeting seconds, long enough for them to ask to see or hear more.

Some great original screenplays could never be explained convincingly to a producer in synopsis form, but not so many as to be a gamble worth taking. If you're already well connected, with a string of successful films or plays to your credit, then you may be able to get potential customers to read complete screenplays. But even then it's still a good idea to use a treatment to judge the reactions you're likely to get and adjust your ideas accordingly.

Start small. Search out the companies that make films for television. Look for independent producers and directors who've done work you like, and try to get to meet them by sending in speculative stuff. They might not give you millions of pounds, but the chances are they will at least let you write the whole thing yourself and not keep bringing in other writers to mess up your stuff.

## Adapting for Different Media

If you have a good idea for a film, ask yourself if the same idea wouldn't work just as well on stage or television or radio. Why limit yourself by aiming at only one medium?

Whenever you prepare a treatment, do as many versions as you can – one for film, one for television, another for radio and another for stage. An idea that could work as a one-off television play or as a series could also work as a fringe-theatre production or a West End show, but each of the four will require a different approach.

If you can adapt your idea as a fringe show that can be produced – perhaps even by yourself and your friends – at very little cost, you've increased the chances of it becoming a reality. Once it's staged as a fringe production you'll have a chance to develop it in conjunction with the performers and the director and you'll be able to test the reactions of the audiences. If the idea is strong enough it will be easier to adapt for a larger theatre and a wider audience. You can invite West End producers to see the play itself (rather than just asking them to read a script), or film or television producers.

## Staying in the Game

You are going to need to put up with a lot of grief from people whose opinions you may not respect, ranging from actors who want to change your lines to money men who want you to write in a part for Bruce Willis. On the whole you'll just have to put up with all of it. You don't want to get a reputation for being difficult. As a writer for television and film you'll always have to work as part of a team.

Be willing to put up with any number of rewrites and be prepared to take whatever work is offered. Of all the branches of writing, scriptwriting is the one that requires the most socialising skills. If you can network you're much more likely to be the first person to come to mind when new concepts are born and discussed. If you would rather hide away in your cottage in Scotland, you'll find it harder to stay in the swim.

You may well benefit from the services of a literary agent for the scripts you're trying to sell, and for commissions like sitcoms or soap operas. Agents tend to know who's doing what and will provide useful introductions. There are many film companies that refuse to read unsolicited material and will only consider something that has come from someone they know, particularly an agent (see Chapter Nineteen).

There are other, more mundane, areas of scriptwriting, like business training videos, which can provide useful practice and will give you experience of working with cameramen and directors.

## Living in Development Hell

Whereas a novelist can usually trust that his or her book will be published once a publisher has agreed to buy it, scriptwriters never know whether their work is actually going to be seen by an audience until it is up there on the screen or the stage. You could sell a hundred treatments and sample scripts and options on other scripts and not one of them would ever make it into production. This will usually be because the people who liked your work weren't able to persuade anyone to come up with the money, or to make space on their schedules or in their theatres. So many pieces of the jigsaw have to come together before it works that the odds will always be stacked against you.

The fact that someone has bought the film rights to your idea or book doesn't necessarily mean that you'll be asked to write the final script. The producer may have a writer they always like to use, or they may not like your style. Equally, they might ask you to write the first draft and then hand that on to others for rewriting. Although it's obviously disappointing, there are considerable advantages to being paid for a product that you need do no more work on.

# CHAPTER EIGHTEEN

# Writing for the Web

*'In the book business all success is really just back pay.'*
Molly Friedrich

When the potential of the Internet dawned on the general public, there was talk about how traditional publishing would soon be a thing of the past. Pundits also predicted that television would kill film, that film would kill live theatre and that radio would be killed by all of them. None of these predictions has come true, and the Web does not look set to destroy traditional publishing, but it does offer the most enormous potential market for the professional writer.

## The Pluses

In the business writing field there are all those websites that need professionals to design and write them. In the magazine field there are the specialist e-zines, catering for just as diverse a marketplace as the traditional printed journals. For fiction writers there is the possibility of downloading your work direct to your readers with minimal interference from publishers and other middlemen.

Stephen King led the way with a novel that he posted on the Net a chapter at a time. He managed to hook over half a million readers, which would have made most of us very happy, though it made him decide it wasn't worth persevering.

## The Minuses

The reason why people logged on to King's work was because he was already famous. He has a huge tribe of loyal followers and everything he does is extensively written about in the media. Everyone knew the book was there. That is the essence of the problem for everyone else. You can certainly put your work on the Net, but how do you steer people towards finding it, when there is so much other stuff already there?

No one has yet come up with a convincing answer to this. The Web is still pioneer territory for writers. Many are managing to find niches into which to sell their material, but most are using it as a way to promote their existing work to a new and bigger audience.

## Be a Pioneer

If you have access to the Internet and time to explore, then do just that. There are a lot of other people doing the same, but this doesn't mean that you won't come up with a market for your work that no one has ever thought of before.

## Is the Web an Infinite Resource?

No, it probably isn't infinite, but we certainly aren't using it to anything like its full capacity yet. The use of e-mails and websites is bound to become more sophisticated and commonplace in the next few years as we all grow more accustomed to the technology, but it may be the niche-marketing potential of the medium which will be most useful to freelance writers.

Say you've written a learned book on the future of Britain's education system. Traditionally it would be marketed by copies being sent out for review and possibly some public relations activity to create controversy. Copies would be stacked up in bookshops (if you're lucky) on the off-chance that people will either come in and ask for it or will spot it as they browse around the shop. This is all very haphazard and deeply reliant on luck.

Supposing, however, you went on to the Internet and found a way of reaching everyone who'd ever registered an interest in education, or who listed their profession as teacher, and you were able to get a précis of the book on their screens with a button to press which would take them directly to an online bookshop, or which would download it directly to their printer.

That already happens, of course, but we're still in the early stages of the system's evolution. Few of us fully understand what's happening out there or how to exploit it most effectively. I'm certain, however, that our basic instincts for rationalisation and organisation will eventually make the Internet as accessible as any library, bookshop or supermarket. We'll establish marketing methods of such precision that every book will be brought quickly and cheaply to the attention of every person who has ever shown or expressed an interest in the subject or the author.

If you've managed to build up a following with one book, and you have a website that your fans pop into from time to time, it will not be hard to sell them another book through the same medium. Stephen King was selling his book just as a television series producer sells future episodes, using cliffhangers, and in much the same way as Charles Dickens sold his stories through popular magazines over a century ago. It's bound to be one way forward for any successful author.

## E-Books

There are already publishers creating books online which customers can download. This is definitely a trend that will grow, but it will probably benefit only authors in certain sectors.

It's a relatively cheap way to publish, so the barriers to entry are low. Anyone can set themselves up as an e-publisher with virtually no capital. It's likely, therefore, that the industry will be flooded very quickly, if it isn't already. Projects like novels will have a very hard time getting noticed among the competition, particularly if most of the famous names are still publishing their wares through the more traditional methods.

If you have a work of fiction that has failed to find a conventional publisher, then an e-publisher could be the next step. But that in itself suggests that all the slush piles in all the publishing houses and agents' offices are eventually going to find their way on to the Net. There aren't going to be enough readers in the world with enough time to make them all successful. But at least they're out there and sooner or later some of them are going to hit it lucky and build a word-of-mouth following which will result in them coming to the reading public's notice.

With non-fiction, particularly reference and school books, e-publishing may prove more fruitful. If a school can download copies of a set text from the Net rather than ordering copies from book wholesalers, they may well do so. If someone is looking for a definitive book on engineering by a professor from Cambridge, they may prefer to spend half an hour online finding it and printing it, rather than going out to bookshops to order it and then waiting anything up to a few weeks for delivery (assuming it's still in print).

Like 'print on demand' (see Chapter Twenty-Four), e-publishing is a great method of production and delivery, but it still requires the same marketing techniques to bring the books to the attention of potential buyers and to alert them as to how they can get hold of them.

# CHAPTER NINETEEN

# Literary Agents – What Are They For and How Do You Get One?

*'Get an agent. Make no excuses for the failure to do so. Get an agent. Otherwise you're a babe among wolves.'*　　　　　　Brendan Francis

Many publishers accept unsolicited work only through literary agents. For the newcomer, finding an agent is even more daunting than finding a publisher. How do you know which are the good ones? How do you convince them to take you on?

There are writer's guides that list all the main agents, most of them based in or near London. The listings usually say what sort of books they specialise in, but the information is very general and won't tell you much. There's no way of knowing whether you're writing to some huge organisation employing dozens of agents or an individual working from home. There's also no way of telling whether they will be the right person for you. (J.K. Rowling chose the agent who eventually took her on because she liked the look of his name; as good a way of choosing as any.)

On the whole, agents do not get involved with the selling of articles, unless it's on behalf of an existing client, or it is in conjunction with a book-publishing project, or it's an investigative piece which is likely to make a great deal of money and lead to other spin-offs. For the amount of work involved with each sale, their ten or fifteen per cent fee just wouldn't be worthwhile for most articles. So you do not need to worry about finding an agent until you want to sell a book or a script.

## Read the Trade Press

Agents do get written about occasionally in the publishing trade magazines. There are columns about who is selling what to whom and if you peruse them for a few months you'll see some familiar names coming round. That doesn't mean that an agent who doesn't publicise their successes isn't having any – many of the most successful never get their names in print at all – but it's a starting point for you.

## Get to Meet as Many Agents as Possible

The best way to judge if an agent is right for you is to meet them, or at least talk on the phone. They will not, however, want to meet you just because you say you're a writer. They're all very busy and time is money to them. They don't need to have hundreds of writers on their books unless those writers have work that can be reasonably easily sold. The chances are they won't want to give you any time at all unless you've already tempted them with a book project they think they can sell. So the first thing you need to do is prepare a project for selling (see Chapter Five).

Once you have the package ready, write to several agents with the synopsis, asking if they would be interested in seeing more or in meeting you. Unless you're very lucky, some of them will ignore your letter completely while others will politely decline your kind offer. Send the sample material to those who are willing to see it and go to see those who are willing to talk to you. Have a career plan of some sort to tell them about. They want to know that you have more than one potential book or script in you and that you're going to be dedicated to promoting yourself as a writer for many years to come.

You may find only one person who's willing to take you on. In which case you'd better go with them for lack of an alternative and think yourself fortunate to have got your foot in the door. If you're lucky enough to catch more than one agent's interest, just follow your instincts. Which of them looked as if they were doing the most business? Which would you trust? Which did you like most?

If you have any contacts in the business, ask if they've heard of any of the agents you've been to see or if they know of anyone else you could ask. Pull any string you can get your hands on.

You'll need to be very comfortable with the person you choose because they're going to be responsible for your career and your income, or at least a major part of it, for some time to come.

## Should You Sign a Contract?

If you want an agent to try to sell your book for you they'll want you to sign an exclusive contract with them. There is no alternative to this; they won't put in any work if they think there's a danger you'll wander off to another agency halfway through the process.

The contracts are usually not too binding. Either side can normally get out of them within a month if they put it in writing. If, however, the agent does manage to sell the book for you, they will always be the agent on that particular project, even if you take future work to someone else. That means that out of anything they earn for you on that project they'll take ten or fifteen per cent before sending the money on to you.

The ideal is to find someone you like from the beginning, someone who makes you so much money that you'll never need to think about going anywhere else. It sometimes happens, and most writers spend many years with their agents, complaining occasionally rather as old married couples might complain about one another, but remaining faithful.

I have to confess I've had a slightly different relationship with agents. Because they quite often come to me with projects that need writers (particularly ghostwriters), I've always fought shy of signing exclusive contracts with any of them. There are several through whom I've sold a number of books and I would be perfectly happy to stay with any one of them exclusively if I were able to get enough work from one source. I have always, however, felt the need to be free to take work wherever it comes from and I've never found an agent who can supply me with a steady stream of projects year in and year out. Sometimes this causes embarrassment, as when a certain famous musician let it be known in the industry that she was looking for a ghostwriter and four different agents rang me up on the same day to find out if I would be interested. I was, and asked the first agent who rang to handle the job, confessing to the others what had happened. I didn't like letting them down, but it was a price worth paying in order to keep myself free.

Some agencies charge a reading fee to try to recoup some income from the hours and days they spend looking at un-solicited submissions from writers, promising to repay the fee should they manage to sell the work. Unless you've been recommended to try that particular agency by someone whose judgement you trust, I'd advise never paying anything. Most of the good agents do not make any charges beyond their percentage of what they earn for you.

## What Will an Agent Do for You?

Agents more than earn their percentage. To start with, they do the selling, probably much more effectively than you could because they can sing your praises unhampered by the need for modesty. In many cases an agent has got me four or five times more for a project than I would ever have dared to ask for myself.

They know what's happening in the market because they're selling all day long, so they're more likely to know which publishers are looking for the sort of book you're selling and how much they're likely to pay.

They'll also be able to haggle with the publishers where you might be too afraid of losing the job. They're expected to be greedy and ruthless. They do it so that you don't have to. They also know that it's in the interests of the publishers to pay you as little as they can get away with, and they're there to stop them. If you're very lucky they'll be able to get several publish-ers bidding against one another for your book in an auction. It would be very hard for a writer who wants to please every publisher on earth to conduct such a ruthlessly commercial exercise.

Then they take care of all the tedious small print, so that you never have to read the contracts at all unless that's the sort of thing that turns you on. They'll spot little things that may well double the amount of money you end up getting. All you have to do is sign where they tell you.

They then do all the chasing up of the money, so that you never have to damage your relationship with the publisher. Any arguing that has to be done they'll do on your behalf. They'll attempt to earn as much as possible for you, so that they in turn also increase their income. It's as simple as that.

Once you've formed a bond of trust you'll be able to use your agent as a sounding board for your future work. They'll know what's likely to sell and what isn't and will sometimes be willing to suggest changes that you can make to a synopsis or even to a final manuscript. You don't have to do as they say, but they're unlikely to give you any bad advice since they have a vested interest in helping you to succeed. It's better to have them tell you the hard truths than the publisher, because once a publisher has said 'no' they're unlikely to change their mind, while you and the agent can do any number of drafts until you're both happy with the product and ready to send it out into the market.

If the agent tells you the project is unsaleable, don't waste their time by arguing. If you strongly disagree, then go to another agent. But if you suspect they might be right, put that idea to one side and start work on another.

## What an Agent Will *Not* Do for You

An agent will not work miracles. If no publisher wants to buy your work there's nothing an agent can do apart from keep trying. If they've been to all the likely potential buyers and been turned down there's little point in you taking it to another agent because they'll have no one else to show it to.

An agent will not 'build your career' unless you have some enormous strokes of luck and are earning so much so quickly that they're able to dedicate their time to you and you alone. Most of the time they'll be scrabbling to sell books for dozens of other writers at the same time as yours. They'll guide you to wise decisions when decisions are needed, but they probably won't be able to spend much time talking about your career in the abstract and they will only occasionally be able to bring projects to you rather than the other way round.

If you have an enormous success with a book everything changes. If you produce millions of pounds in commission they will take very good care to do nothing to slow your career path down or damage your reputation. For the rest of us such a situation is an idle dream. Do not allow yourself to become despondent if getting an agent doesn't change your life. It's up to you to produce great work and your agent will then sell it for you and handle the administration.

Your agent is also not your mother or your nanny or your therapist. If you're earning them enough money they may be willing to listen to your every gripe and moan. If not, you'll soon find your calls not being returned. Save all your personal problems for your friends and family. An agent's time is as precious as a publisher's or an editor's. If you're spending hours on the phone moaning to your agent about the state of your bowels or your need for a new car, you're taking up time when they should be out selling on your behalf. There will be long periods when you hear nothing from them. That's because they have nothing to tell you. Don't expect to speak to them every day, or even every week, unless you're in the middle of a sale or a negotiation. In order not to be feel abandoned and forgotten, concentrate all your efforts on other work.

Once you're a best-selling author you can become a nightmare client and still keep your agent. You can have them running around doing your Christmas shopping, booking your holidays and finding a plumber. Until then, treat them with the same respect you would your lawyer or your doctor.

A good agent can help a writer a great deal; a bad agent can slow down a writer's progress. You do not need an agent to succeed, but any friend and ally you can make in your battle for survival should be treasured.

# CHAPTER TWENTY

# Subsidiary Rights

*'In today's media culture, the actual book is becoming an incidental by-product of a writer's career – something to keep his or her name in circulation.'*
James Wolcott

Think of a book as the seed from which other more profitable deals will grow. As long as you've received enough money from the publisher to cover the time you took to write the book, that's enough to make it worthwhile. What will make it more than worthwhile is the possibility that you'll be able to sell some subsidiary rights.

## Serial Rights

If one of the newspapers would like to serialise your work you'll find the economics of the situation changing radically. You might receive four or five times as much from the newspaper as you do from the book publishers.

On top of that you have the benefit of any publicity the paper gives to the book. There is a possible downside in that some readers may not buy the book because they'll feel they've already read all they want to in the paper, but the chances of those lost sales outweighing the gains in publicity and serial payments is less than negligible.

In some cases, if they're unable to get a serial deal, a publisher will offer extracts from a book to newspapers and magazines for free, because they believe the publicity is worth it.

When your agent sells your book to a publisher they will try to persuade the client to buy it without the serial rights (which obviously means that they will pay less). The agent will then go to the newspapers and try to sell the rights separately on your behalf, which will mean you get all the money (less the agency commission, of course).

If the publisher insists on buying the serial rights, then their rights department will be the ones who will do the selling to the papers. When they get a sale you'll still be entitled to ninety per cent of the money (the percentage might vary according to the deal), but they'll set the advance they have paid you against that. So you will gain because your advance will have been paid off and there will almost certainly be some left over, but you may have to wait for the balance until the book is on the market and the royalties start coming in. It's almost always better to have your agent doing the selling, but sometimes the publishers will make you an offer you can't refuse.

With a very big book that has a strong pictorial content, you might be able to get a double serial deal. When Victoria Beckham wrote her autobiography she was able to sell the serial rights to both the *Daily Mail* and *Hello!*, which helped to offset the costs for both publications and increased her exposure.

## Foreign Sales

A similar situation occurs with foreign sales. Every time you sell a book into a foreign market you increase the amount of money coming in. If a book makes you £10,000 in Britain that's very nice. If it does the same in ten other countries you have a substantial winner on your hands.

Success in one market can lead to success in others. When *Sold* first came out in England it made almost no impact at all. It wasn't until it did so well in France a couple of years later, and almost as well in a dozen other markets, that the British publisher realised they had a potential hit on their hands and relaunched it with a different cover, making it a best-seller in Britain too.

Some agents are better at selling foreign rights than others, having affiliates in any number of different countries. Likewise, some publishers are better at it than others, and your problem is that you probably won't have a clue which of them would do the best job for you. In that situation you'll have to trust your agent's judgement. If you don't, it may be time to think about moving agencies.

There are annual international book fairs in cities including Frankfurt, London and Bologna (the last for children's books only), as well as in America, where one of the primary objectives is to sell as many foreign rights as possible. There are also 'literary scouts' working in every country who are constantly on the lookout for books that they can recommend to publishers in other markets.

Some literary agencies are very honest about their own abilities in the international market and subcontract the foreign sales to specialist agencies in Britain; there aren't many of these.

Foreign sales are a wonderful way to increase your income, but there's little you can do to control them, apart from co-operate with anything anyone asks you to do in the way of promotion.

## American Rights

Often when publishers buy a book they purchase the whole 'English-speaking' world rights, which includes America. It may be worth exploring the possibilities (particularly if you have an agent) of withholding the American rights. The publishers may knock something off the money they're offering, but you might have better luck selling the American rights through your agent than the publisher would have.

## Book Clubs

Book clubs bulk-buy popular titles and produce direct-mail brochures that offer them at bargain prices, advertising their services heavily in the national media. Members of the clubs are obliged to buy a certain number of titles each month, at rock-bottom prices. It's always exciting to find out that one of your books has been selected by a book club because the numbers they order are enormous, and because the advertising in the press makes a bigger impact than anything any publisher is ever likely to do for you.

Quite quickly, however, you realise you're being paid only a few pence (or even a few percentage points of a penny) for every copy sold. One book club might buy two or three times as many copies as your publisher's entire print run for the shops, but the money will not be good. Enjoy the glory of the ads and the numbers, and don't expect to make a fortune.

Those who run the book clubs insist they cater for a readership that would never go into a bookshop, and so they're increasing the potential market, not cutting into sales you might otherwise have achieved at full price. Not all publishers believe them.

## Film and Television Rights and Options

Everyone dreams of selling the film rights to their books. Even a mediocre success in the cinema will boost awareness of a book in the marketplace. Look what the film version of *Chocolat* did for Joanne Harris's book, and there are any number of examples like that. If the film is a big hit, like *Bridget Jones's Diary* or *Harry Potter and the Philosopher's Stone*, then there is no end to the possibilities. For most books, however, the star-studded film premiere is no more than a pipe dream, although that doesn't mean you can't earn money from the rights.

Film and television companies like to own 'options' on properties. That means they will buy from you the rights to make a film or programme from your book for a year or several years. You get to keep that option payment whatever happens. If the film is made during that period they have to pay you another agreed amount. If they haven't succeeded in making the film by the time the option is expired, they have to pay you again if they want to continue to own the option. If they don't renew the option, then you're free to sell it to someone else. Some books continue to be optioned for decades without a single inch of film being shot.

## Audiobooks

The audiobook market is growing all the time. Most best-sellers are brought out on cassette or CD at some stage, with a famous actor or actress reading an abridged version of the work. They can be a useful extra source of income and help to promote the book. Audio sales are usually made by the publisher, but sometimes by the agent.

## Different Editions

If a book is successful it will continue coming out in various editions, each of which will earn you a little more. There are 'large print' editions for the partially sighted. There are 'condensed' editions from publishers like *Reader's Digest*, who will combine a condensed version of your book with others. If you bring out several books in a series they might later come out as an 'omnibus' edition. These sorts of sales are usually made by agents or come about after other publishers approach your initial publisher. There is little you can do to influence sales in this area, so sit back and allow them to surprise you every so often with some good news.

# CHAPTER TWENTY-ONE

# The Money, the Accountant and the Taxman

*'No man but a blockhead ever wrote, except for money.'*
Samuel Johnson

So, how are you going to stay afloat long enough to make a decent living at this game? You're probably not going to make much money in the early stages, and therefore this is the part of your writing career you'll need to plan most carefully. You cannot guarantee that you will earn anything at all for at least a year, maybe longer. So make sure you do not have outgoings that will have to be covered by income from writing. If you have a mortgage you'll have to sell the house and buy something with whatever cash is left, move into a garret, rely on your long-suffering partner to support you or have another part-time job just to cover those payments.

What are the golden rules for this start-up period?

## Enough Saved

Unless you have enough money to survive for a year, you should not give up your day job. At the same time you cannot have a day job which is too demanding of your time or your intellect. It would be better to be mindlessly flipping burgers for a few evenings a week than working as a management trainee in a bank. All you need is enough pennies to keep you alive, so save your grey matter for the important stuff. It also needs to be a job where you're free during the day to meet people and research stories.

## Drawing Up a Business Plan

If you want to borrow money from a bank they'll want to see some sort of business plan. Your accountant, if you have one, can advise you on how to present the information to the bank manager. You may find it useful to draw up a business plan for yourself anyway. It should explain, in realistic terms, how you're going to survive, and address the following questions:

- Who'll give you work?

- How will you persuade them to give it to you?

- How much do you need to earn to live?

- How much are you likely to be paid by your prospective customers?

- How much do you need to spend to set yourself up?

- How long will it be before the money starts to come in?

- Do you have any other income you can rely on while waiting for the money to arrive? How will you be using the incoming money to get more work and increase your earning power?

- What are your goals, both in the short term (say, in a year) and long term (say, in ten years)?

## Cash Flow is King

Always ensure there's more money coming in than going out. This sounds obvious, but it's surprising how many people go out of business by ignoring this rule.

Promises are worth nothing. Everyone may tell you your book will make you a fortune – don't bank on it. When you sell an article an editor may tell you they'll be needing something from you every week – don't bank on it. If a publisher shows an interest in your synopsis and says they'll almost certainly make a bid for the final manuscript – don't bank on it. Until the money has actually reached your bank account or your pocket it is not real, it is just a fantasy. It is good to have dreams, but never bank on them.

Be realistic about this or you won't be able to remain in the business. By all means have some rough cash-flow predictions on money you're owed. And now and then have a wild flight of fantasy and imagine how much you could earn if all your geese turned out to be swans, but do not spend any money until you actually have it in the bank. If you start building up debts you will (a) never pay them off unless you get a second job, and (b) you won't be able to concentrate on your writing because you'll be too worried.

## Making Predictions

If you have some definite commissions lined up from the beginning you'll know what your income is likely to be for the first six months and you can budget accordingly. If you're setting out from scratch you cannot expect to earn anything for at least six months, and you need to know how you will survive for a year on virtually nothing. The chances are it won't be that bad, but you need to know how you would cope if it was. It's no good thinking you'll give writing a try for a few months, because you'll never get it going in time. It requires a long-term commitment.

## How Much Do You Need to Earn?

Ask yourself honestly how much you can realistically hope to earn from writing in the first year or two. There will be months when you can't meet that target, and there will be others where you surpass it, but you still need to know what the bottom line is.

There's no point being too ambitious to start with, because you're going to use this figure to set your rates, and if your rates are too high you won't get any work at all.

So let's say, as an example, that you have decided the minimum you can live on is £15,000 a year. You might there-fore hope to earn £25,000 in the second year. As you will probably have to work at least fifty weeks a year, five days a week, that will mean you need to charge £100 a day minimum.

You won't, of course, be earning every day of the week to start with (although you'll probably be working seven days a week), or you may be doing work which will earn money later but has to be treated as speculative at the beginning. So you need to earn more than this daily rate whenever possible to compensate for the days when you're writing letters, or doing research or spec work.

Without being unrealistic, you should add as much of a margin to the daily rate as you think the market will bear, but it's always better to start low to ensure you get the work in the beginning. There'll be plenty of time for risk-taking later on.

## Being Paid by the Thousand Words

Some editors will ask how much you want 'per thousand'. In most cases they'll tell you what they pay, and you'll just have to accept it, but you'll still need to know what price it's viable to work at. (If the money is less than your basic daily rate, but you will be earning nothing that day if you turn it down, then still accept, because any cash is better than no cash.)

Let's say you hope to write 2000 words a day, but you need another full day to research an article of that length. That will mean you need to be paid as least £100 per thousand words. That's by no means unrealistic at the time of writing and in many cases you would be paid two or three times that rate. As you become more experienced you'll be able to cut down the research time on many of your jobs, until you can do some of them with a couple of phone calls and complete them in one day rather than two, thereby doubling your earning potential. You will also be able to write faster.

What do you do, however, if you're commissioned to write a book of 100,000 words which you think will take you about fifty days to write (at 2000 words a day) and the publisher offers you an advance of £2000? Obviously you hope it will earn you a great deal more in the long run, but supposing it doesn't? At £100 per thousand words you would need a minimum of £5000 to reach your average daily rate on such a project, with no time for research. They're offering you £20 per thousand. You want to take the job, but how do you make it financially worthwhile?

One option is to write very fast indeed (say 4000 words a day), though the quality of the work might suffer, as well as your health. The second is to choose a subject you already have the necessary background material for, to avoid spending time on research. The third is to supplement the writing of the book with other, unrelated, better-paid work such as business and public relations writing. The fourth is to look for other ways of selling the research you're doing on the book, such as articles or public relations opportunities.

What you can't afford to do at the beginning is turn work down, however badly paid it may seem. You need to establish a track record before you can start putting your fees up and being selective about what you take on.

Once a publisher has decided to publish your book, they'll offer you royalty terms, with the advance set against them. Few books will make much money at the beginning of their lives. The chances are a first-time writer will be offered an advance that is little more than an average month's income. It might be as little as a week's income, or as much as three months, but it is unlikely to be more than that.

To make matters worse, the publishers won't pay the whole amount immediately; payments will be spread over as much as a year. If your first book is a success you will be in a stronger position to bargain for more money up front on the next one – but you still won't be able to get very much more.

Every now and then you'll get hold of a story which commands more money than usual, and each opportunity has to be exploited to the full, but the average book does not give you that sort of bargaining power.

## Unexpected Bonuses

Once in a while bonuses will come along unexpectedly. You might, for instance, be able to resell an article you wrote a few months ago (with only an hour or two spent on adapting it) and suddenly add £200 to that day's earnings. Or, if you've written a number of books, you might sell translation rights to one of them unexpectedly and a few thousand pounds arrives out of the blue.

These sorts of occurrences gradually become more common as you get more experienced and increase the library of work you have to sell and resell. Unfortunately, it is at the beginning, when money is tightest, that they happen least often.

When you're starting out the most important of all the golden rules is: '*Keep calm, keep confident and avoid debt as much as possible.*'

## Investing in the Business

As soon as you have funds to spare, invest them in the business. Do you need a better computer? Is there a trip that would give you material to write about? Could you take off a few months to write something more ambitious on spec? Could you invest in a direct-mail or advertising campaign to boost your network of contacts or raise your image? Could you self-publish a pet project that you believe you can find a market for (see Chapter Twenty-Three)? Could you invest in a better website?

## Who Can Help?

Almost no one. Once you're up and running you can hire an accountant, but if you do it at this early stage you'll be incurring another expense when it would be better to spend the money on chasing up stories and buying more floppy disks. If you know any accountants who'll give you advice for free by all means ask them, but they might just tell you the whole idea doesn't make economic sense, because it doesn't. At the beginning it's a leap of faith, but then so is opening a shop, or setting up as a craftsman, or going into any other self-employed, entrepreneurial activity.

You need to start with a few calculations of your start-up costs, which I talked about in Chapter Four. You'll need a room with a comfortable chair and desk, a computer and printer, a telephone, a cassette recorder, stationery and so on. (You don't have to buy these things until you actually need them, but you do need to anticipate the costs and shop around to see where you can buy them most cheaply.)

## Avoiding Trouble

In the early stages concentrate on jobs which are likely to bring money in quickly. If you have a choice between spending the day working on your great novel or working on an article a computing magazine has expressed an interest in, do the article.

Send your invoice in with the work and find out when it is likely to be paid. The moment the money is due, ring your contact or their accounts department and ask if it's on its way. (Better to get on the nerves of the accountants than your contact if there's a choice. You can always go back to the editor later and ask them to hustle the money along for you as a favour.) Ask the accounts people if they need a statement. Some companies have a policy of not paying a bill until a statement arrives. You need to know that, otherwise you may be waiting in vain for them to pay you upon invoice.

Never be embarrassed to plead. Most people will understand if you tell them you really need the money. You can make it into a sort of joke by suggesting you'll be starving to death by the end of the week without their help. More people will respond to cries for help than they will to threats of legal action.

Many companies have set procedures for paying bills, such as not paying until six weeks after publication. It's annoying at the beginning to have to wait so long for your money, but provided you keep a close watch on the figures and survive the first few months, you'll soon adjust to it and it may actually help you to even out your cash flow.

## Expenses

Whenever you're commissioned for a job, always ask if the client will cover expenses. They usually will. If you don't ask you may find your whole fee vanishing into one rail or air ticket or a hotel bill for one night. If overseas travel is involved it would be reasonable for them to make all the arrangements and just send you the tickets. Although they'll be delighted if you volunteer to do all the admin for them, you may not want to shoulder the costs until they get round to paying you.

Keep detailed accounts of every penny you spend in the cause of work and every penny you earn. And keep copies of every invoice and payment slip. Be as meticulous as you can about filing all this junk because one day the taxman will ask to see it, or your accountant will have to charge you for sorting it out.

Anything that's involved in your work can be charged against tax. That means anything to do with the computer you work on, other office supplies and stationery, advertising costs, travel expenses, telephone bills, even a proportion of the lighting and heating bills for the room you use to work in.

Keep these expenses to a minimum. Do not hire an office if you have a spare bedroom that will do. Do not buy a new computer if the one you have is okay. Do not upgrade your car, or travel first class unless someone else is paying, or indulge yourself in any way. (Sorry, but there will be plenty of time to reward yourself in the future, once the money is rolling in.) Never buy rough note pads – you'll have more than enough scrap paper, which you can turn over and reuse.

Try to get things second-hand, or borrow them from friends, or ask for them when it's your birthday or Christmas. It may be that the few hundred pounds you save by scrimping and saving at this stage will make the difference between staying in business and sinking.

Have a rough idea what your regular outgoings will be. However much you pare down your lifestyle, there are bound to be some – food, electricity, telephone bills, travel expenses and so on.

## Keep a Record of Earnings

As you progress you need to keep track of how well you're doing in order to make strategic decisions like whether to do more books and fewer articles, or the other way round; whether you have more success selling over the Net or by post or telephone; whether to concentrate on subjects that can be adapted for film or television, or whether to put most of your time into supplying reliable sources of income like trade magazines. You also need to decide whether you can afford to advertise, build a website, print brochures or put time into a speculative project that is close to your heart.

Keep a record of all money that comes in, and use that as the official total of your earnings. Don't kid yourself you're already earning what you've calculated would be possible if everything went as well as that one good week you had three months ago. Be honest with yourself and only count money that's actually gone into the bank as truly safe.

By the end of the first year you'll be able to see the sort of income you can expect to make in the next six months. You can then see if there has been a month-on-month increase. It'll never be a steady upward curve, but it should show a roughly improving trend.

Add up the total amount you've earned in the previous twelve months. Then, at the end of each following month, work out how much you've earned in the previous twelve months. Keeping a running chart of these monthly 'annual results' will give you a clear idea of what your real average income has been and is likely to become.

If you look at periods of less than a year you'll find the figures too erratic. Some months you'll earn nothing; other months you might earn enough to keep you going for several months. Only by looking at the longer-term trends can you assess your true situation.

By the end of the second year you should be earning at least the amount you hoped to earn at the beginning, and your graph should be showing an upward movement, even if it's somewhat jerky. If you haven't reached that sort of speed by then, you should do some serious soul-searching as to whether you're in the right business, or whether you've got some part of your basic strategy wrong.

## Bad Debts

If you are doubtful about the financial stability of someone who's commissioning work from you, be very careful about what you commit yourself to. Don't agree to undertake a project that will involve you in a great deal of personal expense unless they're willing to advance you some money to cover costs.

If they do go bust, the first you will hear about it will usually be a letter from the receivers telling you you might get one pence in the pound if you're extremely lucky. Forget about it, because you'll never get a penny, and will only waste time and nervous energy fretting about it. Instead, recoup your losses by selling the material to other people. If they've already published your article you won't be able to sell it to any directly competing journal, but you may be able to adapt it.

## Income Tax and VAT

Don't panic. This is not as hard as it looks when you're first confronted by the forms. If you feel the least bit unsure about what you're doing, find a friendly accountant who'll help you without charging a fortune. Promise you'll stick with them once you're rich and famous if they're merciful at this stage; that should give them a laugh!

Once you're earning anything over the minimum tax rates, make sure you put a proportion of everything you earn into an account that will pay the tax bill when it comes in. To have the taxman hanging over your head is a distraction you do not want. Basically, you need to be able to add up all your expenses each year and deduct them from your earnings. The difference is the amount you'll pay tax on. You'll have to pay half your year's tax at the end of January and half six months later. If you're late the tax office will charge you interest. If you're very late they'll become annoyed and your life will be a misery, so don't take any risks.

VAT is slightly more complicated and needn't worry you for a year or two unless you get very lucky. There's a threshold of earnings that you have to pass before you have to register. This changes now and again but is fairly high relative to average earnings. The annoying thing about VAT is that you have to charge your clients for it and then pass the money on. The good thing is that you can claim back the VAT you've spent on your expenses. In the end you should end up the winner because your clients have to give you their VAT and the government will refund you the money you've paid out on outgoings.

If you earn £50,000 in a year, your clients will have paid you an extra £8750, which you pass on to Customs and Excise in quarterly payments, after you have subtracted your outgoing VAT. If you have spent £5000 on expenses you'll be able to claim back £875 (17.5 per cent of £5000) – a useful sum. If you hire an accountant to work this out for you, of course, their fee may well cancel the gain out, so try doing the VAT yourself; it's not difficult and Customs and Excise are very helpful with advice. Do not fall behind with your payments, however, as their reputation for debt collection is considerably more formidable than the Inland Revenue's.

The other advantage of being registered for VAT is that it tells your clients you're successful and professional. Most of them will be registered for VAT themselves, so they'll never complain about paying up because they just claim it back from the government.

## Writing Your Own Pension Fund

People who don't earn very much (which, I'm afraid, is going to be you for at least a few years) cannot afford to pay into a pension fund. That sort of statement used to sound like sacrilege since we were all told that not to provide for your old age was something of a social sin.

One of the most interesting developments of the new millennium, however, has been the revelation that pension-fund managers have no more idea what they're doing than the rest of us; that annuity rates are ridiculously low and that many of us would have done better to have put our pension savings on the dogs.

If you make enough money to be able to put some aside for

your dotage, that's fine, but there's another way of looking at this. Would it not be a good investment to choose a career that doesn't pay very much in the early stages but gradually improves as you (a) get more experienced, (b) become better known, and (c) have more products that are earning royalties from the past.

It's rare for an experienced and hard-working writer to be earning less at the end of their career than at the beginning.

Of course you should save money whenever you can. Of course you should try to buy your home if possible. Of course you should always avoid debt. But do bear in mind that you'll need money much more when you're getting yourself established and bringing up a family than you will once you're up and running, they've all flown the nest and you, or you and your partner, can settle into a smaller home.

Freelance writing has no age limits. Authors sometimes have their books rejected by publishers because they're 'too old'. It's just another way for publishers to say 'no'; no different to saying 'too immature' or 'too middle-class' or 'too old-fashioned'. If you write a good book they'll want to buy it, and your age will be of no more interest to them than the length of your hair or the colour of your tie.

As in any field of endeavour, how much you eventually earn will depend partly on your skill at creating the product, and partly on your ability to manage your time and market your products successfully. If you're good at one of these elements and average at the others you'll survive. If you're bad at all three you need to think of something else to do. If you're good at all three there are no limits.

# CHAPTER TWENTY-TWO

# Helping Publishers Sell Your Books

*'The first rule ... is to have something to say.'* Arthur Schopenhauer

Sometimes it's possible to make a book continue to earn for many years. It should all be part of your ongoing marketing plans (see Chapter Six).

There's a limit to the amount of marketing a publisher can do without your help. They can advertise the book in the trade press. (They won't want to do too much of that because it's an expensive and crowded marketplace.) They can advertise it to the general public. (Even more expensive.) They can handle the physical distribution of the book if there is a demand for it. But that's about as far as they can go without your co-operation.

They'll send a few copies out for review, but the chances of that resulting in something good are small, and there is always the possibility that the book will get bad reviews.

Publishers would much rather generate column inches in the media through interviews with you or articles by you. They would like to hear you talking about the book on the radio and see you lounging on the sofas of the television chat shows.

What your publisher needs from you are:

- Any angles to your personal or professional story that might turn journalists on.

- Any journalists or people of influence who you know or who've written about you or interviewed you before.

- Any special interest groups who might be interested in the subject matter of the book.

- Your willingness to get out there and hustle on their behalf.

No one in any publishing house will ever have as much money, time and effort invested in your book as you have. If you don't become the driving force behind its marketing plan no one else will.

Find out what publications, radio and television programmes and other media the publisher's public relations department are planning to approach on your behalf. Suggest others, and explain why they might be interested. If they don't agree, then make the approaches yourself.

## Suggest Angles

When I published *Maisie's Amazing Maids* I thought that the novel's being based on the adventures of a ghostwriter would be a good angle for journalists. I suggested we send a copy to *Open Book*, a Radio 4 book programme, and they duly interviewed me about the ghostwriting process, mentioning the book several times (and including a reading from *Sold* by an actress). I thought writing magazines would also be interested. That resulted in a three-page profile in *Writing*, including a large picture of the book and front-cover picture of me. None of this publicity would have happened if I hadn't suggested that the ghostwriting angle was a more attractive potential story than the comic and crime aspects of the book.

## Lighting the Fire

Media interest can be hard to ignite but, once the flames have taken hold, it will spread of its own volition. Once a story has been published in a national paper, or you've been interviewed on national radio or television, other media will follow it up. I once wrote a business book which failed to attract any media interest until the *Daily Telegraph* made a story of it. By lunchtime that day I'd received a dozen calls from people in other media who'd seen the piece. They had all been in the original list for press releases and review copies but had not responded. The producer of *Open Book*, who had featured the ghostwriting item, was also producing a series for Radio 3 called *Work in Progress* and asked if I had another ghosted book that I could talk about. That resulted in five ten-minute programmes of me talking about *The Princess and the Villain*.

## Local Radio

Radio stations are a useful source of publicity for writers, having endless hours to fill and virtually no budgets with which to pay professional speakers. If you can offer a topic a disc jockey or journalist feels they can build into an interesting interview they'll respond.

Beware of spending too much time on this, travelling all over the country to spend five minutes on some local station in the middle of the night. If it's going to mean too much travelling time and expense, offer to do the interview over the phone (most stations will be willing to do that) or, if it's a BBC local radio station, ask if there's a local studio you can go into that they can link up with; most towns have one.

Printed publicity material sometimes has a longer useful lifespan than spoken. You may reach a larger initial audience if you appear on a television show, but they may be unable to remember your name or the name of your book five minutes later. With a magazine or newspaper they can keep the article with them until they get round to buying the book, and you'll have a cutting to use as a promotional vehicle for months, if not years, to come.

## Creating New Markets

Publishers will get your book into bookshops and mail-order book clubs. But there may be other outlets useful to you.

On a family holiday in Devon we visited a beach which boasted the remains of a Second World War tank. There was an interesting history as to how this tank came to be there, which was briefly summed up on a plaque. In the car park beside the beach, however, there was an author who'd written a book on the subject. He was standing beside his car and the boot was filled with copies of his book. He was doing a very brisk trade indeed.

I would never have bought that book had I been in a bookshop anywhere else, but because I was on holiday and my interest had been caught by the subject, I was happy to part with a few pounds for a paperback. That author had worked out exactly where his best target market lay.

If you've written a book set on a particular Greek island, contact the country's tourist authority to discuss the possibilities of distribution there. If you've written a book on the importance of fruit in children's diets, contact some fruit and veg shops, health food shops, shops catering to parents of young children, and doctors' surgeries. Do not expect your publisher to have the time for any of this.

The ultimate aim is to create a word-of-mouth campaign for your book. You want readers who already have some interest in the subject matter to tell other people about it. Do anything you can to get it into the hands of people who are likely to enjoy it.

## Be Your Own Retailer

Check your publisher's contract before you start selling your own book in other outlets, but the chances are you'll be free to buy copies at half the retail price and sell them at the full retail price. If you're wanting to sell them into other outlets at wholesale prices you will be acting as an unofficial salesperson for your publisher. In other words you do the selling and use your publisher as the wholesaler-supplier-distributor. That way you won't make any money from your efforts until the royalties start to flow, but you'll still be helping to get the book noticed and talked about.

If your publisher decides your book is no longer making enough money and is planning to withdraw it from the market, you then have an opportunity to buy up the remaining copies at a very reasonable rate (probably no more than a few pence because if they can't sell them to you they'll be passing them to the remainders shops or pulping them). If you feel you can sell a large number, ask your publisher if they would be willing to reprint and sell you the whole print run. You might think you can sell 1000 copies, in which case they'll be able to give you a considerable discount. Bear in mind, however, that 1000 books will take up an awful lot of space until you're able to sell them.

If the publisher has no interest in any of these deals, get your agent to ask them if they would be willing to allow the rights of the book to revert to you. It may be that the rights revert to you automatically once the publisher allows it to go out of print. Once you own the rights you can then think about the possibilities of reprinting it yourself (see Chapter Twenty-Three).

# Self-Publishing

*'You need a certain amount of nerve to be a writer.'*
Margaret Atwood

Self-publishing has changed in recent years. There are now computer programmes that virtually do the job for you. If your computer skills aren't quite up to the job there are plenty of people running small businesses who will do the job for you at very competitive rates. You don't have to do huge print runs any more to get reasonable prices. You can print a few dozen copies of a book or pamphlet almost as cheaply as a few hundred. And then there is the Internet, which allows you to disseminate information to audiences without even having to print hard copies.

## How Does Self-Publishing Work?

Definitions of self-publishing vary, but let's think of it as any project where the writer can sell his or her work to the final reader without involving a middle person like a magazine or book publisher. You might disseminate the information over the Net or by printing a full-scale book or magazine. You are the creator of the product and the distributor and marketer. It seldom leads to big financial rewards, but if you're careful it can be profitable.

A number of authors who have despaired of getting publishers to accept their work have taken this route. Beatrix Potter started by publishing *The Tale of Peter Rabbit* herself and author Timothy Mo started his own imprint when he couldn't persuade his existing publisher to be as enthusiastic about one of his books as he was. When Carl Tighe was unable to find a publisher for his first novel, his landlady decided to become his publisher and the resulting book, *Burning Worm*, ended up shortlisted for the Whitbread Prize. It had reputedly cost just £1000 to publish 250 copies. Jill Paton Walsh, unable to find a publisher for her novel *Knowledge of Angels*, published it herself and reached the Booker shortlist in 1994. Most do not enjoy this much success.

Before you start, find out how much it will cost you if you fail to sell a single copy of the final work. Is that a loss you could survive if necessary?

Work out exactly how you're going to sell the final work and to whom.

Be aware that you are more likely to lose money than make it.

## Market Research

Contact some of your potential customers and ask their opinions. Do some market research.

If you're planning to write a guidebook to your local town, contact some of the shops that might stock it, and the local tourist bureau, and ask them what they'd want to see in the book. Contact your local paper and find out if they'd be willing to promote it in return for some free copies. (They might also be willing to let you use their archives for research.)

If you want to write a history of your old regiment, check how many veterans there are of the same regiment and how you could contact them.

If you run a local village farm shop ask your customers if they'd like a booklet suggesting healthy recipes using the produce you sell.

If you're running a training course of any sort, work out how many copies of a book on the same subject you could sell to people who come on the course, or to those who enquire about it.

Once you've worked out what your core market will be, you

can then think about ways to expand it. The regimental history might well sell through specialist history bookshops; the training book might make a general business-management title that bookshops would be willing to stock (particularly if you managed to get it reviewed in the right media).

## Local Books

Books can also be targeted at local markets. Guides to good pubs and restaurants in a particular area are an obvious example and the genre can cover almost anything from recommended walks to recommended tea shops. Local history books, especially if they include pictures of buildings and streets and views that people recognise, can also find a market. You can distribute them around shops and pubs or sell them from a market stall in your nearest town.

## Doing a Deal with Publishers

If the traditional publishers turned your book down because they couldn't envisage selling enough copies to make it financially worthwhile, you might be able to do a deal with them whereby you guarantee to buy the first 500 or 1000 or 10,000 copies. That will change their calculations completely, their costs will be covered and any copies they're able to sell through the normal channels will be pure profit for them. You'll benefit from their editorial and design skills, their distribution network and the credibility of having their imprint on the spine. You may even make some royalties from the project as well as the profit you make by selling copies yourself.

## Who Can Help?

You may be sufficiently computer-literate to do the bulk of the work yourself. If not, find out who provides what service and how much it's going to cost from advertisements in writing magazines, and lists of people who provide editorial and production services in the writers' handbooks.

Spend time talking to them. You want to find someone you

feel comfortable with. Price will obviously be important, but will they also advise you well rather than just give you a hard sell? If you can build up a good relationship with a book producer it could grow into a full-time business partnership. If you're successful with your format for a guide to your local town, for instance, you might be able to repeat the format for other destinations. Look for potential long-term benefits and mercilessly pick the brains of anyone who's interested enough to talk to you.

## Is it Just Vanity?

Old-fashioned vanity publishers do still exist. They're the firms advertising for authors in the media. When you send them your work they will lavish extravagant praise upon it and make great predictions for its success. They'll offer to publish it for you and will charge you a few thousand pounds for the privilege. Most of them will do a decent job of the design, printing and production but will do nothing about the marketing and distribution. You, consequently, will be left with hundreds or thousands of books and no idea how you're going to get rid of them. You'll have paid out a large sum of money with no business plan as to how you will recoup the outlay.

The golden rule regarding self-publishing is never ask for opinions on the quality and saleability of your work from anyone who stands to gain financially from you. If they do give opinions, disregard them completely. You must reach the conclusion that your work is marketable entirely from solid research and past experience. That way, if you fail to make a profit, it will not be because anyone has conned you or preyed on your vanity.

## Making a Business Plan

Be as ruthless as if you were launching a new brand of baked beans. Find out how big your potential market will be. Be clear in your mind how you'll reach that market and how you'll make the product attractive. Be very precise about the costs and make sure you can afford to lose the money if the project fails. Be certain that you will have the time to do the necessary legwork to sell the final product.

## Become a Media Baron

Magazines can also be self-published, if you see a gap in the market. If you're eighteen you might want something that reviews the best clubs in the area and talks about issues that engage teenagers. If you're a pensioner you may feel your generation isn't catered for in the local media and want to start a publication of your own, addressing all the problems of growing older.

The publication could be for dog lovers in your area, or local retailers or people in need of therapy. It doesn't matter as long as you have material to put into it and a potential audience. It can be no more than two pages long if you want, although it'll obviously make more impact if it's longer. You can produce the first issue as a one-off to see how it goes, printing it out from your computer and selling copies yourself. Or you could commit to producing an issue every few months or every few weeks and build up from there. As well as writing the articles you could also try your hand at selling advertising, or recruit a friend to do it for you.

Your publication might not last past its first issue, but even that will give you something to show to future potential customers. It'll be a showcase for your writing talents and will also demonstrate that you have the drive to go out and make things happen.

Another way forward is to offer to create a magazine for a company, association or other organisation. Many businesses like the idea but lack the manpower to do it themselves. If you can offer a complete package they may well pay you to under-take it. Some in-house magazines can grow into major publishing ventures (the airline or supermarket publications, for instance). The sophistication of these glossy titles doesn't mean that there isn't still a market for a more modest product to suit a more modest backer. You'll have to be able to liaise with the client, do all the costings to ensure a profit and provide a competitively priced service. You'll need to find the stories, write them and get them approved by the client. You'll have to organise the commissioning of other writers if necessary, the illustrations and the design, the printing and production and the physical distribution of the publication.

The more you can do yourself, the more profit will come to you, but you'll also need to know when you should delegate tasks to experts in order to improve the product.

## Create a Website or a Newsletter

If you can compile a great deal of useful specialist information on any one subject, a website or newsletter can be a highly profitable ways of marketing it.

Newsletters are magazines where the editorial is of such high value to the readers that they'll be willing to pay to gain access to it, either on screen or as hard copy. Because the information is of such value, the publisher's incomes do not need to be padded out with advertising revenues. They can make a profit simply by selling subscriptions or by charging for access to the site.

The major selling point for this sort of information is the speed with which it can be updated. It might, for instance, be aimed at the building industry, listing contracts coming up for tender. Any building company that doesn't want to be left behind by the competition will need this information as early as possible to prepare their bids. If a building contract is worth several million pounds, they're not going to worry about paying a few hundred, or even a few thousand, for a service that brings them the necessary information quickly. The same principles apply in any time-sensitive business, from the oil industry to financial services.

As well as the information itself, you'll also need lists of prospective customers to approach.

You'll have to price the product according to the market. If it is a book of specific interest to a small number of people, such as a business reference book or an esoteric art book, then you may have to pitch the price high in order to make a profit, knowing that these customers will be willing to pay. If it's on a more mass-market subject, likely to be bought as an impulse buy, a book of funny stories about cats perhaps, or a book of love poems for Valentine's Day, then it's likely you will have to make it competitive with other books on the market and consequently charge a lower price.

# CHAPTER TWENTY-FOUR

# The Future for Freelance Writers

*'The only end of writing is to enable the reader better to enjoy life, or better to endure it.'*
Samuel Johnson

Things can only get better. People grow hungrier all the time for information and entertainment. We're consuming both at a colossal rate.

Books become cheaper and easier to produce all the time. We can edit on screen in seconds, whereas this used to take days or weeks.

The downside to this progress is that competition gets hotter all the time. A book that doesn't immediately sell disappears from view almost as soon as it comes out. An article might stay online for only a few hours before being replaced by something more up to date.

## Print on Demand

With 'print-on-demand' technology, publishers can produce any number of books within a few days, or even hours. Because they no longer have to commit themselves to huge print runs, they can avoid ending up pulping those that don't sell. (Around 300,000 books a week are destroyed in Britain because publishers were over-optimistic in their predictions.) Surely that practice will end soon and all publishers will start by producing just enough copies to get the book reviewed and into the shops, providing future runs only when the orders come in, controlling their stock as any well-run car manufacturer would control their assembly line.

There are already publishers working on a print-on-demand basis, and this must be the way forward. The advantages to the author are many. It means your book never needs to go out of print because if anyone asks for a copy one can be produced, even many years after it's first published. If, for instance, you're giving a talk in a provincial town somewhere and a dozen people go into the local bookshop to ask for your book, then a print-on-demand publisher will be able to respond, whereas a traditional publisher might by then have allowed the book to slip out of print. If you write an article, or have an article written about you, several years after the initial publication, people will still be able to follow up an interest in you or your subject.

But this innovation only works if the publisher is able to create a demand. While there have been enormous leaps forward in printing and design technology, the science of marketing remains largely unchanged and always unpredictable. A print-on-demand publisher may be concentrating so hard on getting a large number of books on to the market that they will be doing less about the actual marketing. So in the future that burden may fall even more heavily on the shoulders of the author.

## How Could Our Working Lives Get Any Better?

First there was the typewriter, then the word-processor, then the computer. Jobs that used to take us months and require the hiring of a typist can now be done in days. Bulky parcels filled with manuscripts and costing a fortune in postage have been replaced by e-mails that can cross the world in a few seconds. Mobile phones have freed us from being trapped in the house when we are waiting for a call back, or even from being trapped in the country when we feel like a holiday. We can now truly work from anywhere with our laptops and floppy disks. How could it get any better?

We already have to waste less time than ever before on mundane tasks like typing or filing, and soon we'll waste even less because we'll be able to market more effectively and more precisely through the Internet. If you can target 10,000 people who've already shown an interest in your subject matter, why would you need to waste time talking to millions of others who'll never be interested? The scattergun approach to promotion and marketing that has drained so much of our time and energies in the past should eventually become obsolete.

As publishers adopt more print-on-demand techniques, they'll become braver about what they publish. If there is no longer a danger of having to pulp unsold copies they'll be willing to publish more marginal titles.

As the technology grows more sophisticated, self-publishing will become even cheaper and any writer with a good idea will be able to be their own publisher, earning a hundred per cent of the profits instead of ten per cent of the retail price.

Things are just going to go on getting better and better.

# Afterword

So, now you know as much as I do about making money from freelance writing. And within a few years you'll probably have found out all sorts of things I haven't yet thought of, particularly on the world-wide Web, which is creating new opportunities for writers every second of every day. You will invent new ways to market your work and discover new people to sell it to.

If there is one golden rule I would impress on you, it is: 'NEVER, NEVER, NEVER GIVE UP'. Just because your manuscript has been turned down by a hundred people doesn't mean the hundred and first person you show it to won't love it and help you become the next J.K. Rowling or Marcel Proust.

If you are constantly coming up against brick walls, look for other ways to approach things. Always be thinking laterally about new angles, new subjects to write about and new markets to sell to. And always have the needs of the customer clearly in mind before you offer them any sort of proposition. Remember the best way to market anything is to offer it as a solution to a customer's problem (even if they don't realise they have a problem until you point it out).

Success may take longer than you hoped, but once you're up and running you'll find freelance writing the most varied, exciting and satisfying way to earn a living. On the other hand, if you just want to treat it as a useful sideline or hobby, you will achieve many of the same satisfactions and avoid some of the more nerve-racking elements.

Whichever path you choose, I hope you enjoy every step of the journey.

# Useful Addresses

## Magazines

*Publishing News*, 39 Store Street, London WC1E 7DS, Tel: 0207 692 2900, Website: www.publishingnews.co.uk.

*The Bookseller*, Endeavour House, 189 Shaftesbury Avenue, London WC2H 8TJ, Tel: 0207 4206006, Website: www.thebookseller.com

*Writers' Forum*, Writers International Ltd, PO Box 3229, Bournemouth, BH1 1ZS, Tel: 01202 589828, E-mail: writintl@globalnet.co.uk, Website: www.worldwidewriters.com.

*Writers' News*, Yorkshire Post Newspapers Ltd, PO Box 168, Wellington Street, Leeds LS1 1RF, Tel: 0113-238 8333, E-mail: letters@writersnews.co.uk, Website: www.writersnews.co.uk.

*Writing Magazine* (part of *Writer's News*)

## Organisations

National Union of Journalists, 308 Grays Inn Road, London WC1X 8DP, Tel: 0207 278 7916, E-mail: acorn.house@nuj.org.uk

Society of Authors, 84 Drayton Gardens, London SW10 9SB, Tel: 0207 373 6642, E-mail: info@societyofauthors.org, Website: www.societyofauthors.org

Writers' Guild of Britain, 430 Edgware Road, London W2 1EH, Tel: 0207 723 8074, Website: www.writersguild.org.uk

## Websites

www.andrewcrofts.com
www.author-network.com

# Bibliography

Blake, Carole, *From Pitch to Publication* (Pan)

Chisholm, Malcolm, *The Internet Guide for Writers* (How to Books)

Coleman, Vernon, *How to Publish Your Own Book* (Blue Books)

Goldman, William, *Adventures in the Screen Trade* (Abacus)

Goldman, William, *Which Lie Did I Tell?* (Bloomsbury)

Legat, Michael, *An Author's Guide to Publishing* (Robert Hale)

Legal, Michael, *Writing for Pleasure and Profit* (Robert Hale)

Legat, Michael, *Writer's Rights* (Robert Hale)

Legat, Michael, *An Author's Guide to Literary Agents* (Robert Hale)

Legat, Michael, *Writing for a Living* (A&C Black)

Legat, Michael, *Understanding Publisher's Contracts* (Robert Hale)

Lockwood, Trevor & Scott, Karen, *A Writer's Guide to the Internet* (Allison and Busby)

Long, Rob, *Conversations with my Agent* (Faber & Faber)

Scott, Karen, *The Internet Writer's Handbook* (Allison and Busby)

Turner, Barry, *The Writer's Handbook* (Macmillan)

*Writers' and Artists' Yearbook* (A&C Black)

# Index